ARM UP LADIES: HANDGUNS 101 FOR HER

EMPOWERING WOMEN
THROUGH EVERY STEP OF
GUN OWNERSHIP

SUSAN C. CZUBEK

LADIES, I HAVE SOMETHING SPECIAL FOR YOU!

Go to my website handgunsforher.com and follow the links on the page to get these FREE downloadable checklists:

CHECKLIST: TOP 10 QUESTIONS TO ASK BEFORE HIRING AN INSTRUCTOR

Ask these key questions of any instructor you want to hire.

HANDGUN RANKING SHEET

Do a real-time evaluation of any gun you test.

ACKNOWLEDGEMENTS

Thank you to all my early reviewers who struggled through my first draft but provided feedback that kept me on the right track: Carla Thoman, Damion Lupo, Eva Colombo, Keri Moeller, Renee Behinfar, Sharon Allison-Brown, Steve Brown, and Sue Salyers. I especially want to thank Beth Venuti for proofreading.

A special thanks to Jeff Kelly for being my technical editor. You are a true gun enthusiast and the most patient and skilled instructor I've ever encountered. You took me under your wing and taught me most of what I know about guns and shooting techniques.

Sloane Kini, thanks for your coaching and encouragement during the book-writing process.

Finally, I applaud all the women who are driven to be the sisterhood warriors and protectors for themselves, friends, and family.

ABOUT THE AUTHOR

SUSAN C. CZUBEK

Susan has been shooting handguns since 2010. And now she is determined to empower women to protect themselves and their loved ones.

Susan is overjoyed when she sees the confidence shooting gives women, and she's inspired by their stories of survival.

Because she recognizes the difference between being a victim and having a victim mentality, she wants to provide victims with the education and tools to overcome their fears and walk in victory.

Above all she wants people to feel empowered, which leads to confidence, which leads to using one's gifts and talents to serve others.

Susan has worked in the marketing and communications fields since 1998 and has traveled extensively throughout the world. Susan's volunteer causes include veterans and anti-sex-trafficking.

TABLE OF CONTENTS

INTRODUCTION

There's so much to learn about shooting and owning a gun, and you don't even know where to start. You may wonder, Where do I buy a gun? Who will train me? How do I choose which gun is right for me? Where can I go to learn? Will I feel stupid if I ask my questions?

No judgement here. This isn't that place. This is the sisterhood of shooting.

Welcome, ladies! I promise you this isn't going to be a typical gun book, and I hope you're okay with that. This book is for women. Because we learn and communicate differently than men and have different wants and needs, I'll teach you things the guys can't tell you and accelerate your journey to gun ownership. It's the kind of information you won't get from other gun books. You'll get insider secrets like why you should never go from the manicurist to the gun range and how to overcome your fear of accidentally shooting yourself. Oh, come on now, I know you've thought about that last one!

So, if you're a beginner shooter or have never shot before and don't know where to start, no worries. I've been there, done that—I've been shooting regularly for 10 years.

Learn through my stumbles and missteps as I guide you through the process in ways I wished someone would have done for me.

What You Will Learn

You'll tackle fears about owning and shooting a gun and learn:

- how to choose the right gun and get the right training for you

- to enter the range with confidence

- insider tips from a woman who's been there done that

- the unintended benefits from shooting and owning a gun, such as increased confidence and honing in your powerful gift of intuition.

The tips I give you in this handbook will guide you through what you'll need to get started, shatter some of the myths and misconceptions about women and guns, and help you find a community of female shooters from which you can learn and grow.

I'll do this all while telling it to you straight from an insider's perspective, and more importantly from a woman's perspective.

Why You Need This Book

It's 2020 and our country is in civil unrest. How will you defend yourself? I hope you'll never say, "I wish I would have . . ." while hiding under your bed hoping they don't break in.

If you want to overcome a victim mentality or prevent becoming a victim, I want to help you be as prepared as possible and to empower you to be in the best position to protect yourself and your family.

But simply owning a gun doesn't mean you're ready to use it to defend yourself or the ones most important to you. You need to be a responsible gun owner and get proper training and education so you know how to safely use and store your gun, and you know your state's laws regarding firearms. So I cover that too.

This book is written in a way that you can skip around, but let's face it, we're multitaskers and can handle jumping around without getting lost. I may use gun terminology you've never heard of, but you can flip to the glossary in the back for explanations of terms or check online.

I am proud of you for taking the next step in your gun experience! You can do this! I'll meet you where you're at. Let's do this together and have fun! Just a couple of girls chatting it up, like at a happy hour where you get a little tipsy and spill the tea. But what happens at our table stays at our table. That's the sisterhood.

This is your safe place. I am honored to be here with you. I truly am. Let's do this, sister!

PART ONE

EXPLORE FEARS AND MYTHS

CHAPTER 1

FEARS ABOUT GUNS AND SHOOTING

You're instantly jarred wide-awake. You know you heard something. Barely breathing, you strain to listen. Your mouth goes dry and you feel the blood pulsing through your ears. Your heart races and the back of your head breaks into a sweat. Was it just the wind?

OR could it be a crazed thug, hell-bent on breaking into your home, stealing from you, and ruthlessly terrorizing the security and innocence of your loved ones?

This is the time you run through all the nightmare scenarios. What do I do? How am I going to deal with this? Will the police arrive in time? Will I be able to protect my kids?

It's a combined feeling of panic, helplessness, and outright fear.

But it doesn't have to be like this. Why are you trading your power for helplessness?

If fear is what's between you and shooting, let's talk about it. If you have a lot of pent-up fears around shooting and guns, your first time shooting will be scary. But like any fear you have, if you can overcome it, you are on the road to victory.

Fear is powerful. It stops us from doing some things and it motivates us to do other things. Fear sidelined my confidence, but it also motivated me to get back in the game.

When we're afraid, we adopt limiting beliefs. And when we don't believe in ourselves, we often steer clear of opportunities that would allow us to reach our potential. These limiting beliefs prevent us from using our gifts and talents. For example, are you a natural public speaker but lack the ambition to find speaking engagements? Are you good with kids but hide behind a desk? Is there something deep inside you that is calling you to do something bigger, but you've made excuses? Do you have gifts you aren't using? Or hiding? That's fear.

Despite what we have been conditioned to believe, fear is nothing to be ashamed of. Many women experience it.

One of my friends told me about a mind-blowing seminar. The speaker first asked men to raise their hands if they felt afraid at least once in the last two weeks. A couple of them raised their hands. Next, the instructor asked the women the same question. Nearly every hand went up! This was eye-opening for the men, and comforting to the women.

Fact is, in a room of 100 women, there are dozens of reasons women felt afraid in the past two weeks.

Think about the last time you were afraid. Was it walking alone to your car? Or the way a man looked at you? Or did your boyfriend grab you by your wrist during an argument? I want you to really think about it, remember it for a minute. How did your body feel? What did it smell like? What did it taste like?

Now check your heartbeat. Is it beating faster? Do you sense a little anxiety welling up in your throat? That's how fear affects us physiologically. It's uncomfortable. But you can push through your fears. Have you ever heard that saying that you have to face your fears to overcome your fears?

Facing your fears in life—and in shooting—is the first step to moving through them, past them, to the life you want and were meant to live.

When you start taking back some of the ground that fear took, you'll have greater confidence. And, I promise you'll notice that the confidence you gain in one area will translate to confidence in other areas of your life too.

Are you ready to face those fears? I am going to be right here with you, coaching you through this. You can do this! Let's plow through this chapter together.

Face Personal Fears

Talking to many women, I identified four big areas that our fears fall into.

FEAR OF BEING OVERPOWERED

Either you or someone you know has been a victim of attempted or completed sexual assault. If you are a man reading this, you doubt it. If you are a woman, you know it. Statistics vary depending on the source, but one thing the sources agree on is that it is an underreported crime. You confide in your girlfriend, but you don't go to the police. If you were assaulted in any way, my heart goes out to you, and because you survived it, I know you are a strong and powerful woman. If you're having some flashbacks right now, pause, take a few deep breaths and repeat, "I am powerful. I am in control. I am victorious."

Some of us have been pushed around, even beat up by a boyfriend or husband. I am here to tell you your past does not equal your future. Stick with me here, I'm going to help you feel empowered again.

FEAR OF BEING CONTROLLED

Tied closely to that last fear, another big fear we have is feeling like we aren't the one in control. Do you know how to recognize that? You feel angry at the controller and yourself for not speaking up or doing what you know you should. You're not living your truth. Isn't it time for you to be brave?

FEAR OF SOMEONE
HARMING YOUR LOVED ONES

This is a biggie, especially if you are a mom. Society says men are the protectors, but let's be honest mama bears, you know how we can be when we see someone hurting our kids, or parents, or someone else we care about. If you could do something that could prevent anyone from harming anyone you know, you'd do it in a heartbeat, wouldn't you?

FEAR THE POLICE WON'T ARRIVE IN TIME

How long does it take for the police to arrive at your door from the time you hear an intruder and call 911? About 5–10 minutes according to 2019 data collected from police departments by A Secure Life.[1]

Can you fight off an attacker for 5 minutes? How about 10? Are you willing to risk it? Of course not; the time clock on your lives and the lives of your family and pets is ticking away.

You need a way to protect all that is dear to you.

The truth is sometimes the police can't arrive in time to stop a violent attack. Of course, the time it takes police to arrive does depend on a few dynamic factors such as which city you live in, an area's population, call volume, and the number of officers available.

And large disruptive crowds.

In the spring and summer of 2020, people gathered in the streets by the hundreds throughout the country to protest the death of George Floyd at the hands of police officers. They blocked streets and it was hard for police to get through to anyone in those areas who may have needed them.

By May, those protests spanned the country and some turned into riots; businesses were burned and vandalized; people were injured and killed. In Seattle—a hotbed for the riots—a few city blocks were taken over by protesters, blocking the area to city services, including police for a month. After that the group occupied the streets each night while people in nearby homes feared for their safety. Imagine if you could hear chants and smelled smoke from burning buildings every night. Would you feel safe? Would you begin to wonder if someone was going to break into your home?

Residents called 911 desperate for help, but dispatchers were overwhelmed, reported the New York Times in their July 3 edition. Police couldn't arrive in time.

How would you protect yourself and your family if they blocked off your street and the police couldn't reach you?

Then, calls for the defunding of police departments started.

Gun sales soared for months. People who had never thought about buying a gun before armed up.

An NSSF survey reported on Yahoo! News found that 40 percent of gun purchasers during that time were first-time buyers.[2] And 40 percent of those were women, according to Crime Report.[3]

People wanted to protect themselves and not be victimized. Gun ownership is a way to do that.

TAKEAWAYS

- Women experience different fears than men.

- Fear is nothing to be ashamed of.

- Fear can propel you to take action.

Face Gun Fears

Clearly, fear for safety and your life can drive you to gun ownership. But then you may fear learning to shoot. In the next sections, we'll face some common fears and questions that women just like you have toward guns and shooting.

AMMUNITION FEARS

If you drop ammunition (ammo), will it explode? How dangerous is it if you use the wrong caliber? Or if you load it wrong, will it fire backward and shoot you?

I had all these fears and lived with them for longer than I needed to. Geeze, it's amazing I even picked up a gun. How quickly our minds fill the gaps of the unknown with the worst case scenarios. If someone would have addressed my fears as a beginning shooter, I would have been much more relaxed and able to enjoy the experience.

So let's get some of those questions answered for you right now so we can alleviate those fears.

If I drop ammo, will it explode?

Ladies, this is impossible to do.

At the base of the cartridge (another name for ammunition) is the primer. When this is hit, it will fire the bullet. If the primer doesn't get hit, there's no force that will cause it to fire. It's like striking the wrong end of a match—it just won't light. Even if you drop the cartridge on the primer end, that wouldn't be enough force to tap the primer to ignite.

I've seen a few videos of guys putting a cartridge in a vice grip and pounding a nail into the primer end. This is such a guy thing to do! You know what happened? Not much. There was a small spark and a burst. Why didn't it fire? Because it wasn't confined as it would be in the chamber of a gun, so the energy was dispelled. It's physics.

Bottom line, dropped ammo won't explode.

If I load the right ammo in backward, will I get shot?

I blame cartoons for this misconception. Can you picture the one in which the old cowboy character shoots but the gun fires backward? He's left with a smoldering face and the back end of the gun has a gaping hole. Then, the gun slowly goes limp.

14

It's possible to load the ammo backward, and the round will likely get jammed in there so tight you'll get a professional to remove it. It's a safety issue, but, it will not explode nor ignite. Whew! So cross that fear off your list.

What if I load the wrong caliber?

This is a safety issue. It's possible to load the wrong caliber (ammo) and that can be dangerous; it could cause the gun to malfunction and injure you or bystanders. In other cases, it could cause a nasty jam requiring a gunsmith to fix it.

No worries, this is completely avoidable.

When I first started shooting, I checked and triple checked that I was loading the right caliber into the right magazine the right way. I even showed it to my instructor asking if it was right. I wanted that reassurance. I envisioned myself loading the wrong caliber and the gun exploding in my face.

Take precautions like matching the caliber listed on the box of the ammo to the caliber of your gun. Done.

Action steps to alleviate those fears around ammunition

Only set out ammo that's the caliber for the gun you're using

Sometimes I have ammo boxes of different calibers on the counter in my shooting lane because I am shooting different guns that require different ammo. But I didn't do that at first, and you shouldn't either until you recognize the size and feel of the different types of ammunition. The best practice is to only bring out the box of ammo that goes with the gun you're shooting. If you are switching calibers and guns, then put away boxes of ammo that aren't the caliber needed for the gun you're about to shoot.

It's a simple solution that will ease your worry about grabbing the wrong ammo.

Label your ammo box

Here's a fun idea: identify your ammo by attaching colored stickers to the ammunition box. Pink for 9mm, green for .22, blue for .45, and so on. You could even write the caliber on the sticker. Have fun with this—add a splash of color now and then! Not everything in the gun world needs to be khaki green, khaki brown, and black. Ladies, we are naturally creative, most of us anyway.

Check your firearm

Check the caliber for your firearm which is stamped on the barrel of the firearm and on the base of the ammunition. Make sure it's a match.

GUN EXPLODES

You might worry the gun will explode. What if there was so much pressure built up when you fire the gun, that it explodes? What if it fires back at you? What if you got shot in the face?

To understand if any of these scenarios are possible or not, you need to understand how the round (ammunition) fires in the first place. Let's start with the components.

The best way I can help you understand the parts of the ammo is to compare it to something you probably have in your purse right now—lipstick. Stick with me here.

Hold the lipstick in your hand and take off the cover. Pretend that what you're left with in your hand represents the ammunition. The tip of the lipstick is the *bullet*. The plastic around the lipstick represents the *case* of the cartridge, the lipstick inside the tube represents the *propellant*, and the bottom of the lipstick represents the *primer*.

Got that? The bullet is the shaped, exposed part of the lipstick, the propellant is the lipstick inside the case, and the primer is at the bottom base of the tube.

Think of that simple comparison as I explain how the ammunition is made.

The first step in manufacturing is to size the case of the ammo. As there are different lipstick sizes, so too there are different ammo sizes. Next, the primer is pressed into the case (at the base in our lipstick example). The primer must be flush or the cartridge will not feed properly in the weapon magazine, causing a "jam." Then the case is charged or filled with the propellant—in our example, the solid lipstick itself.

Finally, the bullet is inserted in the top. The bullet gets crimped and shaped, like the angled, pointed shape of a newly opened lipstick.

It's a rudimentary real-world example, but I hope it helps you picture the components.

Now that you understand the ammunition components, let's return to the question of whether this ammo is going to explode and hit you.

The simple answer is *no*.

When you properly load the ammo into the gun, the primer side faces toward the back of the gun. When you pull the trigger, a mechanism strikes a firing pin into the primer end, igniting it. That, in turn, ignites the propellant and causes a micro explosion. The high sudden pressure pushes the bullet forward—not backward—and out the barrel of the gun.

When you load the ammo correctly, the bullet won't fire backward because of the mechanics of how a round is fired.

So, no ladies, your gun won't fire backward, you can cross that off your list of fears.

GUN JAMS

A gun jam is a mechanical malfunction in the gun and basically means there's something stuck in the chamber and it needs to be cleared before you can shoot. Don't worry about this, it's happened to every shooter and it's usually an easy fix.

Let me tell you when I first started shooting regularly and my gun jammed, I handed it over like a poopy diaper to my instructor.

Didn't want anything to do with it. Wasn't my problem. I was afraid to deal with it.

At first, I lacked the upper-body strength to pull back the slide of the 9mm I was shooting so that was my excuse. (The slide is the top part on the gun that moves back, exposing the chamber and any ammo that gets trapped.) I figured my weakness would buy me some time in my training. But my instructor was on to me, and he brought a .22 to our next training session. That's a smaller caliber and the slide is super easy. He handed it to me, and now I had to pray it wouldn't jam. And it didn't. Whew. I was in the clear! Oh, but not for long.

He reached into his bag of tricks and pulled out a box of blue ammo. These are practice rounds, he explained. "I want you to get used to what it feels like when your gun jams, and I want you to know how to clear a round." Noooooo!!! What if my finger gets caught and crushed? What if I am not strong enough to keep the slide back and it slips out of my fingers and fires the bullet?

He loaded the magazine with some blue rounds. This was cruel. Despite my apprehension, I faced my fear and fired it. Okay, felt normal, and then another one, and another one. But then, on that fourth one, it felt like I shot a cap gun. It sounded lighter and felt lighter.

He touched my shoulder and told me to pull back the slide to release the round that jammed. Um, what? This was my moment. All eyes were on me. Actually, only my instructor's eyes were on me, but it felt like the pressure of a lot of eyes on me. I figured I could at least give it the 'ole college try. I rotated my right wrist so the gun was leaning more sideways, just like he showed me earlier. Then, I reached over with my left hand and pulled back the slide. And out popped a blue round! That was easy! He helped me face the fear of the gun jamming.

Sure, I could do it with a practice round, but what about a live round? Gulp.

It's important to know how to shoot, but equally important to know how to clear a non-functioning round from the chamber.

My instructor that day was Jeff Kelly, the best instructor I've ever had! Ladies, if you hire an instructor, it's so important that you get one who helps you overcome your fears. Jeff pushed me outside my comfort zone a lot and gave me the confidence to do it.

We did that drill with practice rounds mixed with live rounds for the next 10 minutes. I never knew when the practice round was coming, but when it did, I felt it and heard it. And I knew it couldn't hurt me.

I felt good about this. Next session he brought 9mm practice rounds and a 9mm gun, of course. The pop was bigger, but it was still a hollow sound. It doesn't take as much strength to clear a practice round, so we repeated the drill. At the end of the drill, I was confident I could clear the practice round anytime it came up. So, for the next few sessions, we spent 10 minutes alternating blue and live rounds. I was feeling good. Confident.

Tip: When you pull back the slide to pop out the jammed ammo, angle it downward as far as you can, using gravity to your advantage, and pop out the round.

Reasons why guns jam

Guns jam for two reasons. One reason you have more control over than the other.

Your gun needs to be cleaned

When I was young, my dad taught me to always put something back where you found it and to take good care of everything. I was a daddy's girl, and even though I had two brothers, I'd tell my dad I was the son he never had. I loved following him around when he was fixing things around the house, or painting, or doing dad stuff. He made sure I knew the importance of getting regular oil changes in my vehicle, cleaning tools when I'm done with them, and repairing anything right away that's broken. So naturally, when I learned that a dirty gun is one reason your gun jams, I thought, duh, that's never going to happen to my gun. But the other reason? Well, I couldn't fully control that.

You have bad ammo

My mentor taught me there are times when you need to spend the extra money to get better quality. Like when you're heading to an interview. That's the time to invest in some solid heels. (I also learned from him that guys look at your shoes more than you know!) You want to get shoes that look sharp but are comfortable and made by a reputable brand.

Think about it. You could spend $40 on a pair of black heels to go with your smart interview outfit, but you know they're cheap and oh, so uncomfortable. They don't make you feel at the top of your game. You dread wearing them again, so you buy another pair of

$40 shoes for the next interview. Now you're out $80 for shoes you may not wear again versus investing in one pair of high-quality, comfortable shoes—shoes that cause you to want to be the hot seat so you can wear them again!

Just like shoe quality varies, so does ammo quality. The lesson here? Don't buy cheap ammo! Buy ammo with a solid reputation. You may spend more. That's OK. When you're first starting, you want to stack the deck in your favor. Do things that build your success and your confidence. If you skimp on ammo and every 15th round is crap, and you need to clear a jam, how fun is that? Not!

When you start taking your newfound skill seriously and want to embrace shooting as a hobby or sport, then you'll go through a lot of rounds, and you can decide if cheaper is worth it. But for now, pay for quality.

Tips for clearing jams

Never put your finger in that rectangular opening (chamber) that appears after you pull back the slide. Okay, I have an icky story for you.

I was on the range alone—this was sometime after I learned how to clear a jam. Well, my gun jammed. I did what I was supposed to do, pulled back the slide, tilted it, but it wouldn't budge. I mean this sucker was in there good. I wanted to walk away, and I was a little embarrassed that I couldn't clear it. But I know you can't walk off the range with a loaded gun, so I had to fix this.

I looked back and motioned for the range officer stationed at the back of the lanes to help. By the way, range officers can be super helpful. The safety of the range is their responsibility, so if someone needs help, they want to help. Let's face it, those bravado male officers want to help women shooters with things like clearing a jam.

Anyway, he grabbed the gun and had problems too, and then he did what you should never do. I'm feeling queasy thinking about it right now. He put his finger in the opening to dislodge the round. It worked, the round angled up, but the slide jammed his finger. He turned to me and helplessly held up the gun to me with his finger lodged. Clearly, he needed help and was counting on me to do it. I quickly reached over with two hands on the gun and pulled back the slide, and he immediately withdrew his finger. Oh, that had to hurt. Yikes. Bet he lost a fingernail on that. Ladies, don't do this.

You can buy tools to clear jams, or you can bring a wooden dowel from home with you. If it's jammed in there that good, I highly recommend you have someone with more experience get it unjammed. Oh, and tell them to watch their fingers!

Takeaways

- Newbie shooters should buy new, manufactured ammo, not handmade.

- Ask for help when you need it.

- Never put your finger where it doesn't belong.

SHELL CASINGS HIT YOUR FACE

When I was 19, my best friend and I traveled throughout Europe. In Greece we took a local train. It was dilapidated and packed with locals going about their business. All of us were sweaty from the overbearing humidity and lack of air conditioning on the train. Though every window was down to let some circulation in, the windows were the kind that lowered only to the halfway point of the entire window.

Ahh, finally, the train picked up speed and that breeze felt good. Throughout the countryside, the cicadas, as if angry at the soaring temperatures, let out loud buzzing noises that pierced our ears. Soon after the train picked up speed, tiny projectiles were hitting me in the face, in the arm, nearly in my mouth! I was getting pelted by buzzing cicadas flying in through the window! I ducked and dodged, but took several to the face. I wasn't left scarred or bleeding, but it stung a little.

While I didn't love that moment, I survived. So when you shoot and shell casings hit your face, just think of them as annoying cicadas. You too, will survive and soon it won't even phase you. Shell casings are the part of the ammo that ejects when the gun is fired. It's like the rocket thruster that falls back to earth after launch. But since they do not have the velocity of the bullet, you have very little chance of getting scarred or bleeding. Just kidding, there is almost no chance of this. But, just in case, this is why you wear eye protection, girl!

If you continually get hit in the face, then it may be an issue of not holding the gun correctly. It could be that you need to tighten your grip so it doesn't dip. Hmm, that's catchy. Tighten the grip so it doesn't dip.

Tip: Your initial reaction when you're hit with one of these may be to reach for your face. But remember, you have a gun in your hand that should always point downrange! Do not forget that. Keep the front of the gun (muzzle) pointed downrange.

ACCIDENTAL FIRE

Ok, unless you're in a Stephen King movie, a gun isn't going to fire all by itself. Even if it's loaded, it still won't happen—unless there is a fault in the gun itself. I don't know of anyone this happened to and only put it in here to reiterate this: treat every gun as if it's loaded and could accidentally fire and always point it in a safe direction.

You may be wondering why you hear about guns accidentally going off if this only happens if the gun is defective. I know you've heard stories of someone cleaning their gun and it accidentally fires. (Tragically, there always seems to be a toddler who gets hit—see my chapter on kids and guns). Oh, it's an accident alright, if you define an accident as doing something unintentionally.

But most of the stories you hear are due to negligence, not accidental discharges. Negligent discharges are caused by unsafe behavior with a firearm. Basic safety is covered in another chapter, but a few examples would be leaving your firearm loaded in an area where unauthorized persons (kids) can access, resting your finger on the trigger instead of the trigger guard while waiting to shoot, and storing your concealed gun in a way that the trigger catches and fires.

Carrying in your purse

I've established that if the gun is just lying there, it's not going to fire, but what if it's in your purse? Yes, you can carry a gun in your purse.

Same thing, it can't fire unless the trigger is pulled. With that said, when you are choosing a gun for the sole purpose of concealed carry (this simply means you are in public and have a gun on you or close to you, such as in your purse), be sure you consider the inside of your purse. This is not a time to be a hoarder. The best safety scenario for purse-carrying is to use one that has a separate compartment where you store your gun and nothing else—no gum, hairbrush, tampon, wallet, nothing it can get caught on.

If it happens

If you are in a situation where a gun unintentionally fires, this is a wakeup call. Assuming no one is hurt, this is a warning you cannot ignore because you may not get another one. Immediately assess why the gun fired. If it was because of someone else's actions, talk with them about what happened. Express the seriousness of the situation and then put safeguards in place where you either are never around this person again with firearms, or you have a come-to-Jesus talk with the person about safety.

Don't just say, "Whew we were lucky" and move on. Ask why it happened. What can be done to prevent this? Do I want to be around this person again when there is a gun around too?

If the unintentional fire is because of something you did, I feel for you. It is a sick feeling. What can you do in the future so this never happens? Do you need a gun safety course?

An accidental fire can even make you walk away and never shoot again. But you can prevent this if you focus on safety first. Safety should never become routine. If you are a checklist person, then carry a checklist around with you. Never go on autopilot around firearms.

Having a gun is a responsibility. We are not perfect, and accidents can happen. But let's do everything we can to prevent them, okay?

I'M GONNA GO TO JAIL

You want to be a law-abiding citizen and stay out of jail. So, it's natural to ask, What if I have a gun and do something wrong and get arrested? Who's going to take care of my kids?

Some women I talked to said they want to know the law before they even pick up a gun. Bravo, we need law-abiding gun owners.

I didn't understand practical law and guns when I started. Most confusing to me is that states can make their own nuanced laws and these vary from state to state. So make sure you know the laws in your state, and then you can avoid this. You also need to know the laws for any state you plan to travel to while carrying your gun.

If I drive across the border from Arizona to California, one of the more restrictive gun law states, then I better be sure I know the laws there.

Do you drive to Mexico for vacation? A lot of Arizonans, Texans, and Californians do. What if you have a gun in your vehicle when you cross the border? Oh, hell no; don't do this. They don't take kindly to people bringing guns into their country. I would even be sure you don't have any ammo, a gun cleaning kit, or anything that indicates you own a firearm if you're driving across the border. It's a little different if you are going in with a gun for hunting, but even then, you need a permit in advance. In many countries, it's illegal to bring in firearms and ammo.

How about heading to Canada eh? Laws are more lenient there. If you have a rifle for hunting and it's hunting season, you just need to declare it at the border and pay a fee. Generally, you are not allowed to carry handguns for self-protection in Canada. Always check the government website of the state or country you are traveling to in order to learn the laws.

Tip: Don't travel using a bag you've ever placed ammo or firearms in because at the very least if the TSA swab shows gun powder, you will be questioned and delayed, or if you're in another country, you may be detained.

AT THE RANGE

A range is a place where people go to shoot all sorts of weapons and ranges can be indoors or outdoors. The noise and just being at a range can all be a little scary. And you don't want to look stupid. Well, I am here to help!

You may want to do a little recon before you go to the range for the first time to put your mind at ease. Head to the range or gun club—you can walk right in, you don't need a membership to enter. Go to the retail area, not the actual firing lanes. Think of it as shopping that will calm your nerves; plus, while you're looking at the fashionable concealed-carry purses, you can get used to the continual popping sound coming from the range. Yep, those are guns firing. Don't worry, the retail area is in a safe area, so you're not at risk of getting shot. But you will hear the faint sounds coming from the shooting lanes. It can be a little unnerving if that's your first time hearing that.

And you'll see people with guns which can be even more unnerving.

If you have never seen someone carrying a gun on their waistband or seen guns on walls or in the display cases, the whole experience could cause a little anxiety. If you think it will, go to the range first. Most have places you can sit, so go sit. Get used to the sounds and the sights.

The first time I saw someone open carry, I was in a completely different country. When I was 19, I took a teaching job and lived in Hamina, Finland, 30 miles from the Russian border. My Finnish co-teacher took me horseback riding at the ranch where she boarded her horse. It was just a few miles from the border. Then she took me right by the border check. Just 30 feet from me, several Russian soldiers carried rifles. I was scared. I'd never seen anyone carrying a rifle like that in public.

Several countries have mandatory service in the armed forces. Russia is one of them but a few countries on that list that may surprise you—Finland, Switzerland, Denmark, and Sweden. Women in these countries are used to seeing people carrying and using firearms, but in the US we're not.

So, if you have never seen a gun out in the wild, definitely go to the range or club first to ease those first-time fears.

CHAPTER 2

FEMALE GUN OWNER MYTHS AND MISCONCEPTIONS

"Come on, honey, let's go to the range, and I'll show you how to shoot." And so begins the awkward and frustrating story of how many women are introduced to shooting.

The man in your life wants to show you how to shoot, but he usually steers you to a gun he likes—something that is tried and true for him, but it may not be the right gun for you.

These well-intentioned men in our lives don't understand our fears around shooting and don't have a clue how to give the insider tips that a woman cares about, nor do they understand female shooters' unique needs.

Besides those close to us making assumptions, gun consumer culture finds it easy to stereotype female gun owners as a group, leading to a lot of myths surrounding female gun owners.

ALL WOMEN WHO SHOOT ARE SEXY

Just look at your movie role models—Women who are gunslingers look like Angelina Jolie in Mr. and Mrs. Smith, and Jolie as Lara Croft in Tomb Raiders. Or Halle Berry as "Jinx," a Bond girl. The message is if you're not sexy, you shouldn't shoot.

But can shooting make you sexy? People are attracted to people who are confident and some say that is sexy. And when you shoot, you will gain confidence. Does that translate into sex appeal? These are things that make you go hmm.

True confession—sometimes shooting does make me feel sexy. It's a combo of power and sexiness. Like when I'm shooting and my groupings are tight (shots are close together on target). Or when I fast shoot 12 rounds, calmly set down my gun, and take a deep breath, like I just slayed the biggest giant. I can sense the guys around me staring at me. Maybe this isn't a myth afterall!

YOU WANT A PINK GUN

It starts at birth—boys are blue; girls are pink.

Since the gun industry started paying attention to the rising demographic of females interested in gun ownership, manufacturers produced pink guns. Then came the clothing, range bags, and even ammunition. Somewhere someone in an executive office decided that all women want pink guns and accessories. They thought it would be pretty and that would sell.

Today, you can get pink, purple, Tiffany blue, and even custom paint jobs for your guns.

It can seem more fun to shoot a colored gun, and it certainly brightens the range to have gun colors other than silver and black.

However, some argue that brightly colored guns are a problem because a child in your household could think it looks like a toy, you may not be taken seriously, and it draws attention to your concealed-carry gun.

As female gun owners became more sophisticated, we demanded more out of guns than color. Don't let anyone stereotype you into buying a pink gun. If you do get a pink gun, do it because it's the right gun for you.

In the end, your purchase should be weighted heavily on the ergonomics, functionality, and reliability of the gun.

A WOMAN WILL BECOME
A VICTIM OF HER OWN GUN

Whether that means she will be injured because she doesn't know how to operate it or she will be overpowered by a criminal who will use the gun against her, many believe a woman is destined to become a victim of her own gun.

GIRLS DON'T SHOOT AS GOOD AS GUYS

Guys in a gun store or range are fun to watch. They become giddy like girls, but at the same time their chests poof out like the hulk. Fascinating.

Once when I went to the range with a couple of guys, I watched as they were salivating as they peered into glass cases teasing them with guns they wanted, couldn't afford, and would never buy. They dry-fired (pulled the trigger of an unloaded gun) a few and swapped stories about their alleged experiences with the guns. I think it's some kind of routine I haven't figured out. Maybe it's like us when we're shopping with a girlfriend and we bond over shoe shopping. Ooh-ing and ah-ing over Jimmie Choos and Christian Louboutin, knowing we'll never get them—but it's so nice to imagine.

Impatiently, I bought a few targets for us and time on two lanes. Let's get on with it already. We're on our lunch break after all. I felt like the husband sitting in the chair holding a purse outside the dressing room, checking his watch to see how much of the game he'd already missed.

Finally, we headed in. Gary and I were in one lane and Mike was in the other. Gary and I took turns shooting. I got bored and walked to Mike's lane. I didn't know Mike well—I'd talked to him a few times in the office and overheard him and Gary whispering over YouTube gun videos.

I batted my eyes and asked Mike what he was shooting. He told me and asked if I would like to shoot it. He reloaded the magazine and handed it over. That was awful gentlemanly of him. I grabbed

34

it and rapidly fired at the target. Boom, boom, boom, until I emptied the 12-round magazine. My grouping was tight, and with a smirk and a gleam of thrill in my eye, I calmly laid the gun on the table, turned to him, and said, "That was fun." Mic drop.

He never expected that from a girl.

Men seem surprised and intimidated when a woman shoots well. Only a man with a healthy ego can appreciate a woman who can shoot as well or better than he shoots.

They never asked me to go shooting again.

Given that we have a different physical makeup than guys, we also have to deal with the physical-based assumptions.

YOU NEED A SMALL CALIBER AND SMALL PISTOL

Men are floored when I tell them my favorite gun to shoot is the 1911. The 1911 is a .45 caliber and looks like a badass. It has serious stopping power. By the way, stopping power means it will stop an attacker or intruder in their tracks.

The first time I shot the 1911 I was at an outdoor range. I wasn't expecting to hit the target with it, but I did. I hit the bullseye! There's a certain satisfaction when you hit the bullseye. It felt perfect. I tried again and hit it. This gun was crazy accurate for me!

Any chance I get, I'll shoot the 1911. It's tried and true. I am a bit of show-off at the indoor range with it. I very calmly load it, raise it, shoot it. Fast fire. Tight grouping, inside the red. Then, I calmly set it down and sense the men next to me, jaws dropping. How can someone who's 5'2" shoot this thing? How can a *woman* shoot this like she does?

But as much as I love it, I don't own a 1911. Want to know why? It's not the right gun for me.

It's too big for my need. My purpose for owning a gun is to have a conceal-carry gun and another for protection in my home. After fast shooting 10 rounds with the 1911, my hand hurts, and I can feel that I don't have a tight grip on it that I should in order to use it safely in a stressful situation. If the grip gets wet from sweaty palms in a stressful situation, that could be just enough moisture to make my grip insecure.

I hate to admit it, but the 1911 is too much gun for me. God bless you if you have big hands and decide this is the gun for you. I will be envious.

Does that mean I should jump to a .22 caliber pistol? No, it's a myth that a woman, because she's a woman, should settle for a smaller caliber just because it's a smaller gun with minimum punch.

The misconception is that all women have small hands so they will all want a small gun.

A .22 would fit my hand size, but does it fit my purpose? No, it doesn't. I want a gun with stopping power. My attacker may be pumped with enough adrenaline that if I shoot him with a .22, he'll keep coming at me. I want a gun that gives me enough time to get away or to stop my attacker in his tracks.

So, ladies, don't think you're stuck with a .22.

Size matters, or does it? I mean come on, ladies. We all know, it's not the size of your gun, it's what you can do with it.

Remember that time you were invited to a party and you didn't have a thing to wear? And then you remembered your little black dress. Although you're not so little anymore, it still fits. A little snug, but it's the best dress for the occasion. Now thankfully this wasn't the who's who of the year event or you'd have plenty of critics saying that your dress didn't fit. But what they don't know is how it makes you feel. Snug schmug. You still look fabulous! And that makes you confident. And in the end, it's the not size of the gun or the caliber that matters, it's the confidence you have when you use it.

We see it all around us, every day. Media, people, and friends all like to point out why we can't do something rather than why we can. Focusing on why we can't do something reminds us that we haven't done something yet. But it doesn't mean we can't do something.

You are different, yes, but not *inferior* because you are a woman.

Filmmaker Cathyrn Czubek summed up female gun ownership perfectly when she commented on her documentary *A Girl and a Gun*:

> The classic Hollywood portrayals of pistol-packin' mamas, tomboy sharp shooters, sexually twisted femme fatales, and high-heeled, cold-blooded assassins are caricatures. In truth, the typical woman who hangs out at rifle ranges and keeps

ammo in her purse is the girl-next-door, the single mom, a hard-working sister or aunt. Maybe she's a realist or has learned tough lessons from life; either way, she cares about her personal safety and may even find salvation, comfort, or something satisfying in possessing a gun. In a word, she is empowered.

PART TWO

EDUCATE

CHAPTER 3

WHY DO YOU WANT A GUN?

The reasons women choose to bear arms vary. Some are concerned about personal safety so they're being proactive, while others have already been victims of crime and want to prevent it from happening again. Still others enjoy the thrill of competition or the sisterhood found among other women in the gun world.

Owning a gun is a very personal decision. It's not up to your significant other, your dad, or your best friend. Owning a gun is up to you.

Being a gun owner is also a big responsibility and it's not a decision that should be taken lightly. You're taking an important step right now by educating yourself.

When you become a gun owner, you are joining the sisterhood of thousands of women in the US who own a firearm. The National Rifle Association (NRA) reports a rise in female gun ownership from 13 percent in 2005 to 23 percent in 2020.[4]

Regardless of your *why*, gun ownership is your right as long as you pass the background checks. So if you have decided you want to buy a gun, you need to answer *why*.

What will you use it for? Protection? Fun? Competition?

According to the Pew Research Center, on average, women who currently own or have owned a gun report that they first got their own gun when they were 27 years old. For me it was at age 37.[5]

If you know your reason, think of it as you read. If you don't, don't sweat it; read on and you may just decide on your reason.

Common reasons for owning a gun include

- Self-defense

- Home protection

- Recreation

- Competition

Protection

Most women, around 92 percent, say protection is one of the reasons they own a gun; in fact, 27 percent say it is the *only* reason they own a gun according to a 2017 Pew Research study. You're a woman, you were born with the instinct to protect and nurture. If you have kids, you know exactly what I am talking about. A quiet, petite mother can go full-on mama bear when her kiddos are threatened. When you do that the first time, you'll look around and say, Who is this woman? You were taught to fall in line, not to question because the teacher will handle it, your husband will take care of it, the police will help me. That's why when you go mama bear for the first time, it kind of freaks you out.

But it shouldn't. Why wouldn't you do everything you can to protect your loved ones?

Earlier, we covered the four big fear areas in our lives. They all revolve around our safety.

How many times have you been alone on a street or in a parking lot and the hairs on the back of your neck stand up when you see a man in the distance headed toward you? Your senses went up. You were sizing him up without even knowing it. Inside, your reptilian brain assessed whether he was a threat to you. You noted what he was wearing, how he was walking. As he approached you, your heart rate increased, you went through scenarios: if he talks to you, if he stops, can you run in the shoes you're wearing, if you scream can anyone hear? As he approached, you noted he looked sketchy. You wondered what you had on you that you could use to defend yourself with. Keys? Nail file? Maybe your mind even flashed to a recent report of an attack or a memory of being attacked yourself, and all these thoughts and experiences bubble up your fear. Then he got closer, just 10 feet away. He was looking at you, something in your gut was uneasy. He passed you; you take a deep breath. Suddenly, he twisted your arm behind you and wrestled you to the ground.

How this ends is, in part, up to you.

You see, protection starts well before you step into that parking garage or onto the sidewalk. It starts with admitting to yourself that it could happen to you and then deciding you want to do everything you can to prevent becoming a victim.

You need situational awareness—awareness of your surroundings.

Women have an intuition that we need to trust. If you've ever come out of a situation and said, I knew that was going to happen, or I had a bad feeling about it, or the hair on the back of my neck stood up, etc., that was your intuition at work. I think intuition is more than the woo-woo. Intuition results from all the data your brain is processing through all your senses without your being consciously aware of it. It's like having a second brain that compiles all the data and spits out a conclusion which results in a feeling, which we label as intuition. I think women pick up on non-verbal cues better than men, so we pick up on all the aggression signs, and it causes us to be in a state of heightened anxiety, fear, and awareness.

If you want to learn more about how to be more aware of these cues, I recommend the *Gift of Fear* by Gavin de Becker.

Women are usually physically weaker than men, but that doesn't mean we need to succumb to being a victim. At the very least, please take a self-defense class to protect yourself.

Studies show that aggressors identify their target by how the person moves, how aware they are, how confident they appear. Do they want to attack someone who holds their head up and shoulders back or someone who looks at the ground and looks meek?

Learning to shoot—even if you never own a gun—can help build confidence that transfers to the street. There's something about learning a new skill which naturally builds confidence; plus, you're in the driver's seat—you are the one in control. This can be super empowering.

Besides building confidence, we have something we know how to use to defend ourselves.

HOME PROTECTION

Even when you get a gun for home protection, it's ultimately for self-protection. This is where I started. I had a dog and an alarm, but still, I heard stories of people breaking in. And can I count on police getting there in time? Let me tell you what happened to me.

In my twenties, I lived in a single-level home with my roommate and her two dogs. I came home after work and parked in the carport (for those who have no idea what this is, it's a spot in the driveway that has an overhang or roof, but no walls). Anyway, I put my key in the lock and turned. The first thing I noticed was that the dogs weren't there to greet me. I noticed this, but I was on autopilot so I didn't sense the danger. I had done this routine for two years. I set my purse on the counter, and then just had that feeling. Something wasn't right. I passed by the living room on the way to my room and saw the dogs in the backyard and the back gate was open. In my head, I thought, this isn't normal. But I was in motion and walked down the hallway, and the first door on the right was my bathroom, and the small window was open. That wasn't normal. But still, I wasn't in that fight or flight mode. The level of danger hadn't registered.

I kept walking like the dumb teen in one of those B-rated horror films. I slowly opened the door to the left of my room. I didn't remember shutting the door, but I must have, right? I walked into my room, it looked fine. Suddenly I sensed fast movement behind me and a chill went throughout my body like an electric current. I turned around and then froze. All my senses were on high alert. I saw nothing but heard the outside door slam. I walked quickly back to the living room in time to see someone run into the alley through the open gate.

Now they had my attention. Could there be someone else in the house? The thought was terrifying. What would I do if there was?

Absolute fear gripped me and ripped me out into a hollow shell. I felt a rush from the head to my feet. I bolted down the hall toward the door to the carport and over to my neighbors' home. I asked to use their phone and called the police. (This was back in the day before cellphones!)

An officer came and went inside the house while I anxiously waited outside. Then he called me in to go room to room to check if anything was missing. My room was untouched. My roommate's room across from mine had clearly been ransacked. The thief ended up stealing her passport and some jewelry. The burglar must have been hiding in the third bedroom and ran out as I stepped into my bedroom!

The officer said I must have startled the burglar and that I was very lucky that he ran out of the house.

Very lucky indeed. What would the burglar have done if I had gone into my roommate's bedroom? It makes me sick to think about it. I could have been attacked and I had nothing in my hands to defend myself with. No keys, not baseball bat, no gun. No protection.

With the way things are today, many are looking for ways to protect their home.

May 25, 2020, we saw how quickly the city climate can change. That was the day George Floyd died while in the custody of the Minneapolis police. May 26, protesters took the streets in Minnesota. The following night, protesters were marching in the streets of other major US cities. The tension escalated quickly. People set fires to buildings and cars, looted businesses, and tagged buildings. It was all hands on deck in law enforcement ranks.

Residents near protest areas were told to stay indoors, with many also realizing they are on their own. Streets were blocked off and all eyes were on the protesters, vandals, and looters. It was mayhem in many cities. Cars were burned, bottles were thrown, and people were murdered.

Can you imagine how frightening it would have been to be a regular citizen going about life and be caught suddenly in the middle of this?

In some cities, such as Chicago, officers worked 12-hour shifts to help deal with protests and looting while all days off were temporarily postponed, according to city Superintendent David Brown. With all the officers trying to quell protests and looting, shop owners were left to fend for themselves, some stationing themselves inside their stores with guns on hips, ready to defend their businesses.

Besides the rise in violence and looting, you know what else spiked? Gun sales. Whether out of fear or necessity, record gun sales were recorded in May, according to the 2nd Amendment Daily News. Many were first-time gun owners.[6]

Then Fox Business news reported, "Approximately 1,726,053 guns were sold in May—a record-breaking 80.2 percent increase from last year, according to data released late Monday by Small Arms Analytics & Forecasting, which examines the raw data obtained from the FBI's National Instant Criminal Background Check System, or NICS.[7]

"Of the firearms sold, 1,052,723 were handguns, the SAAF [Small Arms Analytics & Forecasting] estimated."

With all eyes on the protesters and rioters, who was going to protect you? In times like those, you are your own first responder and must be your own protector of your home or business.

Frankly, sometimes the police don't have enough time to respond before disaster strikes. It will be up to you to protect yourself. What will you do? What are you prepared to do?

As I am writing this in the summer of 2020, the majority of Minneapolis Council members want to disband the police. There are calls for disbanding or defunding the police in cities across the US.

This is a terrifying notion for the vulnerable, law-abiding citizens in our population.

PROTECTION AGAINST AN ACTIVE SHOOTER

Lt. Colonel Dave Grossman said, "If you don't teach them what to do, you teach them to do nothing. If you don't teach them what to do, in most cases they will freeze and they will do nothing and they will wait for their turn to die."

Sounds like he's talking about our soldiers and Marines, right? Nope. Lt. Colonel Dave Grossman was referring to our school kids.

Do you realize our kids are likely more prepared for a mass shooting that us?

One way we can be prepared ourselves is, ironically, learning to shoot.

During a 2020 episode of the PonderMed podcast, Grossman describes our conditions of readiness. He says that if you never think anything bad is going to happen to you, you are in condition white. These are the moms going around saying, not my kid; these are the people who live a very protected life. What a great state would that be? So peaceful, rose-colored glasses and all. Problem is when you are in that state and something bad does happen, you are unprepared to act. You can easily become a victim.

Grossman, a former US Army Ranger, paratrooper, and psychology professor, describes coping strategies for the physiological and psychological effects experienced under the stresses of deadly battle in his book, *On Combat: The Psychology and Physiology of Deadly Conflict in War and Peace*.

When you are fighting for your life, you enter condition black as in battle. This is where cognition doesn't register and you are just reacting to survive.

Lt. Grossman said our goal should be to live in condition yellow, a state of readiness.

Much like the state of ER doctors and nurses who perform in circumstances that would make most of us want to curl up and hide in a corner. But they've conditioned themselves to function at a high level in stressful situations. They have seen this before. Same with our soldiers and Marines.

People like ER healthcare professionals and our military forces can function as yogis. They recognize what's going on around them, but they don't freak out because they have seen this before in training and real life. Some have an eerie calm as they go about doing their jobs. They control their breathing and heart rate and other physiological factors.

Let's go a little deeper into this so you can understand why learning to shoot conditions you to be better prepared to survive a mass shooting.

There are two divisions of our autonomic nervous system—the **parasympathetic nervous system** and the **sympathetic nervous system.** We'll call them the lizard brain and the yogi brain.

The lizard brain is raw, real, and reactionary. The yogi brain is controlled, calculated, and concentrated.

Lizard mode has an involuntary impact on the nervous system, heart, breath, visual and auditory perception, and memory. It's what kicks in when fear and self-preservation take over. Ever heard of fight or flight? That's the lizard talking.

Imagine if a gunman were to storm into wherever you're at—your car, your home, your office. Without training, you'll immediately go into lizard mode—into a reactionary state of mind.

If you've been training at a range, you've become conditioned to recognize gunfire, and you can balance your lizard with the clarity of reaction that comes from being a yogi.

RUN, HIDE, FIGHT

When we see, do, or hear something for the first time, it causes a certain level of anxiety or excitement. The first time you hear gunfire, it may cause fear because it's so loud. You may have a faint smell of gun powder and grime. You may have been close enough to feel a percussion.

When you reach the point that gunfire doesn't cause you to freeze or be gripped with fear, you will be able to use your yogi brain.

In a mass shooting, the time you go from shock and reaction to consciously acting can mean the difference between life and death. You can reduce the lag time by recognizing that there is a gun being shot in public.

Without training when you hear gunfire so many things could go through your mind. How many times have you heard someone say they thought it was a car backfiring? By the time your brain acknowledges that it could be gunfire, you may have lost precious seconds. So you need to learn to recognize it quickly.

The FBI identifies three reactions to a dangerous scenario such as a mass shooting—run, hide, and fight.

A person initiating an unprovoked shooting does not have good intentions. So you must immediately get in the mindset that this person wants to hurt others and you. This isn't the time to think the shooter will stop, won't come after you, or that you are a victim. This is the time to run, hide, or fight.

You've seen the horrific videos of people running from a shooting with their hands in the air as police crouch. They run.

It's a natural reaction to want to escape danger. If that seems like the best option for you at that moment, then run like your life depends on it, because it may.

You later learn of the terrified people who hid under a desk or in a closet. They hide. Sometimes, the best option is to hide. If you can hide in a closet or barricade yourself in a room, then that's what you do. However, if you choose to hide, you still need to be prepared to fight. What if the gunman discovers you?

And then, sometimes you hear about the heroic actions of a person who tackled the gunman. They fight. As a last resort, the FBI recommends fighting. Fighting may be throwing objects at the gunman; it may mean wrestling the person to the ground. It may mean using your gun.

Your training and experience empower you to make the right decision for you at that moment. Knowledge is power. If you recognize the sounds you hear as a gun you can quickly decide if you want to run, or take cover, or fight. Without that knowledge you won't immediately recognize it, and instead of rising to the occasion, you'll fall to your level of inexperience.

After you recognize and are comfortable with the sound of a gun firing, you'll get to the point that you can recognize the caliber. This is important in an active shooter situation. If you can't see the gunman but can only hear the shots, knowing which weapon is being shot will help you decide what to do. Hearing a handgun versus hearing an automatic rifle affects your response. If there are lapses in shooting, you can guess that the gunman is reloading or moving. This may be a time to run. A rifle can kill more people faster. It causes more destruction.

Depending on what you hear and your level of confidence, you may decide to go on the offensive to save lives.

Gunmen count on people's fear. I think they get off on it. If you fight back, that is unexpected. Mass shooters are cowards.

If you recognize the sound of gunfire as a gun and *not* a car backfiring, you may have just bought yourself a few extra seconds. You can react immediately rather than looking around to see how other people are reacting. Maybe you can recognize the gun is jammed because you've experienced that yourself, you know what that sounds like, and you know how long it takes to clear the jam. Is that enough time to run? To hide? To fight?

If you end up fighting, you will know how to drop the magazine. This could buy you time, and at the most, the gun has only one bullet to fire. You also know how to put the safety on, or can recognize when it's not on.

Of these three initial reactions—run, hide, fight—which one do you think you would most likely choose? Would you like to be in a position to have the knowledge and experience to open you to options?

The more experience you have, the more knowledge you have, and the better equipped you are to make the right decision for you and for the circumstance.

So be prepared. I think everyone, at the very least, should go to the shooting range several times to become familiar with the sound and smell.

It may just save your life.

I hope I am never in a mass shooting situation. But I know I have the knowledge to recognize what's happening, and I hope I have the presence of mind to act smartly. You need to do the same.

Be a yogi, not a reptile.

Recreation

Another reason you may buy a gun is for recreation. Several. It can be a fun activity. North of where I live is an outdoor shooting range called Ben Avery.

My friend invited me to a belt-fed machine gun match at another outdoor range east of Phoenix. The belt-fed is about as mechanical of a gun as you can get, a lot of engineers enjoyed it. It's a beast. At the time I hadn't shot one before. It's a very physical experience. The gun sits on the ground, so you must lie on the ground to shoot it. It was noisy. It was dirty. These guns are decades old, stemming from WWI.

Learning to shoot any gun opens you to a whole community of gun enthusiasts. You may start with the handgun but may find your passion lies in the belt-fed beast.

Competition

Women compete in the 10-meter and 25-meter pistol in addition to skeet, trap, and rifle events in the Olympics, but you can also participate in local clubs and events.

I went to a three-gun match at an outdoor range. These guys—and most were guys—were intense. This was a sport, a hobby, a passion for them. Each shooting stage is designed with a theme and a lot of thought goes into this. Not surprisingly a lot of western themes are used; after all, it is in Arizona.

CHAPTER 4

SAFETY

Safely using and storing your gun is a key component of being a responsible gun owner.

Top 8 Gun Safety Tips

It is best to be overly cautious when dealing with a gun. Make sure you always, always follow the common gun safety rules and never get lax about them.

1. KEEP THE MUZZLE
POINTED IN A SAFE DIRECTION

Never point at anything you don't intend to shoot. This is a good practice whether your gun is loaded or not. When you're shooting with others, this tip is for safety and courtesy. You may know your gun is unloaded, but the person next to you doesn't. No need to cause them to fear for their safety or go into a panic when the barrel of gun points in their direction.

2. FIREARMS SHOULD BE UNLOADED WHEN NOT IN USE

Always unload your weapon when you are done shooting, whether at an indoor or outdoor range. If you hand your gun to someone else, check to be sure it's not loaded, and likewise, if someone hands you a gun, check its status—loaded or unloaded?

3. DON'T RELY ON YOUR GUN'S SAFETY DEVICE

Some say having a safety device on a gun is worse than not having a safety because it gives you a false sense of security. Like anything mechanical, the safety may malfunction or you may think it's on when it's off. It's something to think about when you test guns to find the right gun for you.

4. WEAR EYE AND EAR PROTECTION

Ranges require this and it's for your protection. Shooting is loud. Loud enough to permanently damage your hearing if you're not wearing protection. And you should always protect your eyes— casings from the ammo will eject and fly backward, sometimes hitting you in the face like those cicadas I told you about earlier.

Eye and ear protection are commonly referred to as eyes and ears.

As long as we're talking eyes, let's talk about glasses at the range.

You need to wear eye protection when shooting—doesn't matter if you are at an indoor or outdoor range—safety glasses are a must. You also need to be able to see close and far away. You need to see close to load your gun and read the electronic device to move your target at an indoor range, and you need to see far to see your target and beyond.

My near-sightedness has gotten worse in the last few years. I was okay with readers and gradually went from squinting to read my text messages to reaching for readers. Then I got to the point where I needed glasses for seeing most things close.

My near-sightedness has now gotten bad enough to where I can't see the display on the electronic box in my lane at the range that controls target distance.

What do you do if you wear glasses and not contacts? I know some people who use prescription safety glasses. You can wear your safety goggles over your glasses, but it can be cumbersome. You'll want to figure that out before you go shooting for the first time.

5. KEEP YOUR FINGER OFF THE TRIGGER UNTIL YOU ARE READY TO SHOOT

Sometimes you may want to point at a target with your gun to check the sight or get yourself ready. However when you do this, never put your finger on the trigger—rest it outside the trigger guard with your trigger finger pointed forward.

6. BE SURE OF YOUR TARGET AND WHAT'S BEYOND IT

At an indoor range, if you're firing at your target in your lane, this isn't an issue. Where it becomes an issue is if you are at an outdoor range. Be sure you know what is well beyond your target and beware of anything near your target that could ricochet the bullet.

7. USE CORRECT AMMUNITION

Check your gun's instruction manual and the ammo you are loading to be sure it's correct. Firing incorrect ammo can result in damage or destruction to the gun and possible injury to yourself.

8. DON'T HANDLE YOUR GUN WHILE UNDER THE INFLUENCE OF DRUGS OR ALCOHOL

You should not handle your gun in any way when you're under the influence of a controlled substance. This includes showing it to a friend, cleaning it, and above all, shooting it.

Storage and Safety Devices

Where and how you store your gun is another safety consideration. Safe storage of firearms refers to devices that limit gun access to those you haven't been authorized to use your firearm or those who are prohibited from possessing a firearm. What qualifies as a secure gun storage or safety device? Let's go right to the ATF's definition:[8]

1. A device that, when installed on a firearm, is designed to prevent the firearm from being operated without first deactivating the device;

2. A device incorporated into the design of the firearm that is designed to prevent the operation of the firearm by anyone not having access to the device; or

3. A safe, gun safe, gun case, lockbox, or other device that is designed to be or can be used to store a firearm and that is designed to be unlocked only by means of a key, a combination, or other similar means.

Note that zip ties, rope, and string do not meet this definition!

Let's explore examples of storage and safety devices that you can use to secure your firearms.

EXTERNAL LOCKS

External locks, like cable locks and trigger locks, are devices that secure your gun and are usually used when your gun is outside a safe.

These inexpensive solutions provide minimal safeguards for your weapon. A cable lock passes through the weapon and prevents the firing mechanism from working, while a trigger lock fits around the trigger and trigger guard to prevent it from firing.

The level of security on these reminds me of that of the lock that comes with some suitcases; it's extra security to keep your bag closed, but if someone from TSA wants to get into, it's easy for them to do so. Essentially, it will keep your gun safe from your kids, but not safe from an adult.

Cost: $8–$15.

SMART GUN TECHNOLOGY

The idea with any smart gun technology is to render the firearm useless for anyone except the designated user. There are some really cool advances in technology and gun safety in two areas of smart tech: biometrics and radio frequency identification (RFID).

Biometrics

One version of biometrics is fingerprint access technology in the form of a device that attaches to the gun and looks like a holster. To access the gun, you lay your finger across the scanner to unlock and release the gun. The company Identilock claims the fingerprint technology on their products works as fast as the blink of an eye. These run about $90. Some biometrics technology can store the fingerprints of multiple users.

Advantages are obvious: a toddler who gets a hold of a gun can't shoot it, nor can a criminal if your gun is stolen.

This type of tech is already being used on smartphones and building access pads.

Another type of biotechnology is grip recognition technology that measures muscle tension in the handler's arm to determine if it's the authorized user. This hasn't hit the mainstream yet.

RFID

Clothing retailers commonly use RFID chips to reduce theft and real-time inventory tracking, and now this technology is being used in the gun world.

With RFID, information is shared between objects through electromagnetic fields and radio waves. Tokens are manufactured that can be worn as a bracelet or dog tag rendering the paired gun unusable unless the token is within close proximity to it.

I geek out on this stuff and so does The Smart Tech Challenges Foundation, an organization dedicated to the development of gun safety technology.

While these advances in technology aren't widely available, they have the potential to build a bridge between proponents and opponents of gun ownership in four ways:

- Keeps guns from being used by children and those wishing to harm themselves.

- Disrupts the market for stolen guns because once the criminal has the gun, they can't use it.

- Prevents officers' guns from being wrestled from them and used against them.

- Smart technology doesn't directly infringe on the Second Amendment.

If smart technology isn't available or you'd rather not use it, you can turn to traditional cabinets and safes for storage of firearms.

CABINET

A cabinet is more of a gun display or a simple storage device. Cabinets tend to look nice and are made of wood or thin metal, but can be easily breached. A cabinet is better than nothing, but the construction is not as secure as that of a safe.

Cost: $100 and up. Prices vary greatly from a single metal cabinet to a beautiful wood and glass showcase.

SAFES

Gun safes are made of steel, come in a range of sizes, and some are fire and waterproof.

If you want the peace of mind of having your gun nearby you at night but want to secure it away from your child, consider a small bedside safe.

An app can control some models, some have fingerprint or electronic access, and others use standard lock and key or combo lock for access. I like the concept of an electronic keypad entry, but I've read too much about Electromagnetic Pulse (EMP) interference to rely on this 100 percent. I would feel safer with one that had a dual lock system where it could be opened with a manual dial if the electronic one failed.

The price range on small safes is considerable. Be sure you read reviews on safes, especially where speed of access and quality of construction are concerned.

Cost: $100–$2,000

If you want a little more security, get a safe that bolts to the floor, an in-floor safe, or one too heavy for a thief to carry.

When you get a safe, think of what else you'll put in there. Do you have jewelry, documents, or another gun? Will you buy more guns in the future?

Large gun safes are good if you have long guns, such as shotguns or rifles, but bad if you need to move them. You'll probably need to hire a safe shop or moving company to move them.

Cost: $2,000+ Expect to pay a few thousand dollars to start for a tall safe.

PLACEMENT

I hear people bragging about the guns they own or having a safe out in the open. To me, this is inviting trouble. I recommend keeping your safe out of sight and keep your bragging to a small group of trusted friends.

Tip: Have a light source by and in the safe like a stick-on battery-operated light in case your electricity is out.

LAW FOR LOCKING UP GUNS

Check with your own state's requirements. As of this writing, only Massachusetts requires firearms to be locked in a container. If you live with someone who can't legally possess firearms, additional laws regarding the securing of weapons apply in other states. When children could gain access to your firearms, additional laws apply and are too nuanced and beyond the scope of this book. Please practice due diligence and check with your own state's legal requirements.

Cleaning

A dirty gun can negatively affect the safety and performance of your gun. The barrel of your gun can get gunked up because of the grime on the ammo, carbon buildup, and dust that creeps in over time with regular use.

You can buy a gun cleaning kit that has the tools and instructions you need. When you clean your gun for the first time, do it with someone who is experienced in this area, just so they can give you some pointers and make sure it all gets done correctly.

If you have a revolver, you're at an advantage because you have fewer parts to clean.

You do need to be certain the gun fires again after it's reassembled, so check the functional firing using dummy rounds.

Tip: Many indoor and outdoor shooting ranges have gun cleaning services. Many times these cleaning services are free for members.

HOW OFTEN SHOULD I CLEAN MY GUN?

Just like you get regular oil changes for your vehicle (you do this, right?!) to maintain longevity and performance, you should regularly clean your gun for the same reason.

There are a couple of different types of cleanings—a wipe down and a full breakdown cleaning of each part of the gun.

How often you do either of these depends on what the gun is being used for and how often you're using it.

If you are using your firearm for competitive shooting or self-defense, you want to give yourself every advantage—that gun needs to fire every time. Most sources say you should do a full breakdown or "field strip" cleaning after every use in these cases.

If you are shooting for recreational reasons, you still need to clean your gun, but you could get by with wiping down parts instead of a full breakdown cleaning after every use.

If you notice your gun is jamming and it's not due to a change in ammo, it may be due to a buildup of grime. If you notice performance and reliability issues, your gun is overdue for a cleaning!

Finally, never clean your gun with a kiddo in the room unless you are training them to clean the gun as part of educating them on gun safety.

So many things can go wrong: they can distract you or jump on you trying to get attention. When you're distracted, you miss things; you're not concentrating.

Speaking of kids, let's talk about kids and guns next.

Kids and Guns

According to Pew Research Center, nearly all gun owners (95 percent) believe that talking to children about gun safety is essential. Followed by 66 percent who say all guns should be kept in a locked place when children are living in the home.[9]

I don't believe in hiding your in-home gun from your kids, pretending it doesn't exist. Kids are curious, and whether or not they know there's a gun in the house, there's a chance they'll find it. If you have a gun in your home, introduce your kids to it in stages, depending on their maturity level. The NRA has a good article on age appropriate stages. They suggest starting basics around age six. Later on, teach them how to handle and shoot.

Demonstrate the seriousness of owning and handling a gun. Tell them and show them by your actions.

Start by showing your kid what the gun can do. Take them to the range. Get them to have a healthy fear and respect for what they could do with the gun.

If you live in a house that has guns, I think everyone in that household that's age-appropriate should know how to handle a gun and know basic gun safety.

Even if you don't have a gun in your home, your child may visit a home that has a gun.

They should understand what to do if they ever come across a gun because if you don't teach them, that curiosity could lead to a deadly encounter. Clearly, if your kids don't know the proper handling and treatment of a firearm, they could kill or endanger themselves or others. So teach them early, and then secure your firearms to protect their safety.

For more on kids and gun safety, check out Julie Golob's book, *Toys, Tools, Guns & Rules: A Children's Book About Gun Safety.*

Shooting While Pregnant

I searched to give you some solid information that included studies and stats about pregnancy and shooting, but I didn't find a lot of data except from the EPA. I assume there isn't much research because only a small percentage of women who are pregnant shoot so the research priority is low.

However, we can make deductions based on numerous studies on the effects of lead and noise on children and adults. From that data, we can infer there are two inherent dangers of shooting while pregnant: lead and noise!

LEAD

There's lead in ammo and lead exposure can harm you and your baby.

Lead affects adults' blood pressure, nervous system, and muscle and joint pain.[10] So it makes sense that it can have the same effect on a baby in the womb. Some studies show it can affect brain development and birth weight of your baby. The EPA says lead accumulates in a mother's bones over time and is released during pregnancy and can pass to the baby. This can cause behavioral problems in the child or can put the mother at risk for miscarriage.

LOUD NOISES

According to the American Speech-Language-Hearing Association (ASHA), hearing loss can occur at 140 dB and the sound of gunfire is at or above that level.[11] While sounds are muffled in the womb, it's likely not enough to protect the hearing of your baby if you are at an active range. It may cause stress to your baby too.

If I were pregnant, I would pause live shooting based on that information. However, consult with your doctor because ultimately this choice is up to you.

If you still want to shoot, go to an outdoor range so you're away from other shooters, and use a silencer on your pistol. Also, wash your hands and clothes immediately afterward and wear a mask to reduce lead exposure.

For more information about shooting while pregnant, I recommend Julie Golob's e-book, *Shooting While Pregnant*.

Gun safety goes beyond securing your weapon. It's how you act when you have a gun, and it's in the training and education you get.

CHAPTER 5

LAW—WHAT YOU NEED TO KNOW

It's important to know the law to protect yourself as a gun owner and to be a good gun citizen.

Second Amendment

The Second Amendment of the United States Constitution states,

"A well-regulated militia, being necessary to the security of a free State, the right of the people to keep and bear Arms, shall not be infringed."

I didn't think researching gun laws in America would help me educate haters on Facebook about the Second Amendment, but it did.

During the riots following the death of George Floyd, a friend posted on Facebook a story about a jewelry store owner who got his buddies together—armed—to hole up in the store to protect his property. The group of rioters saw them, made a few remarks, and moved on. As Facebook goes, snarky comments ensued about being armed.

Friend of a friend: *Ironically, the Second Amendment has nothing to do with personal protection from private citizens. It's about being able to defend against tyrannical government.*

Me: *That's how it was written; however, through the years, it has been further defined. The 2008 case of District of Columbia v Heller holds that "the Second Amendment protects an individual's right to possess a firearm unconnected with service in the militia, and to use that firearm for traditionally lawful purposes such as self-defense within the home."*

I sounded smart, didn't I? Citing a legal case and all?

That brief interaction was another example of the many myths out there about lawful gun ownership.

Did you know 74 percent of gun owners say the right to own a gun is essential to their freedom according to Pew Research? And 35 percent of non-gun owners say the same thing. This according to their June 22, 2017 report.[12]

I learned about the Second Amendment long before I started shooting, thanks to a constitutional law class I took in college taught by a passionate professor.

At the university I attended, your class grade was partially based on attendance. Professor Alan Bigel announced that it would not be part of his grading system and that he intended to teach a class that was so interesting people would want to come to it. And he did. Day after day his class was packed.

Miraculously, he made the Federalist Papers interesting. The Federalist Papers were essays written to urge New Yorkers to adopt the Constitution over the existing Articles of Confederation. They explain provisions of the Constitution in detail. Wait, don't yawn off. Its authors, Alexander Hamilton and James Madison were members of the Constitutional Convention. Because of that, the Federalist Papers are often used today to help interpret the intentions of those drafting the Constitution.

Perhaps that's what guided the Supreme Court in their 2008 decision that I referenced in my Facebook post, which I found on the Legal Information Institute's page.[13]

Another day in the spring of 2020 wasn't a good day in court for those in California seeking to restrict the Second Amendment. April 23 a judge overruled the California law requiring a background check on the purchase of ammo, saying it violated the constitutional right to bear arms. The restrictions were put in place a year earlier.

A US News and World Report article states that four states—Connecticut, Illinois, Massachusetts, and New Jersey—require buyers to undergo background checks to get an ammunition license that they must show for every ammo purchase. These may be challenged given the California ruling.

Note: The Gun Control Act of 1968 stipulates that no handgun or ammo could be sold to someone under twenty-one years old.

MEDIA'S FEAR-MONGERING CAMPAIGN

While the Second Amendment is alive and well, it has been threatened through a lack of understanding and fear-mongering. I used to work at a TV station—just a local one, not one of the fancy-schmancy big network ones. We tried to get our stories accurate, I mean that's a sign of good reporting, right? I paid close attention to the language used surrounding guns and shootings and can see how the media shapes views on guns and gun ownership.

Words matter. For example, consider how a change in wording can shape your opinion and perception.

Which sounds more frightening—an AR-15, or a military-style assault rifle?

Some argue that citizens shouldn't be able to own ARs. Yes, if you can legally own a firearm, you can legally own an assault rifle. However, there are more hoops to jump through to purchase—you are required to be ATF approved, pay a special tax, and your name goes on a separate government list.

When the media reports that an AR was used in a shooting without explaining that it was or could have been legally owned, it paints a criminal picture.

And when it's reported that a gun isn't registered to the person who has it, you think that gun holder must be a criminal, right? Having a gun not registered to you doesn't make you a criminal. In Arizona, you can buy a gun from a friend and not have it registered in your name. Sometimes the media reports the gun was unregistered and implies that it's illegal, even though it just might not be in that person's name because they got it from a friend.

Each registered gun has a serial number. An unregistered gun is one with a serial number removed and is a whole different matter. There's only one reason to sand off your serial number—you're going to commit a crime and you don't want the gun to be traced. But sometimes the media will use the word *unregistered* even when it is registered, instantly targeting the person as a criminal. This adds to the misconception that citizens all have nefarious reasons for owning a gun.

Another way the news shapes negative bias toward firearms is when reporters make a big deal about the amount of ammo or weaponry found in houses.

With headlines like "Man arrested after police discover thousands of handgun and rifle rounds in home," people who don't understand how many rounds is normal for a gun enthusiast think this is a crime in itself.

When I shot pistols for review for this book, I shot three magazines per gun. So, somewhere between five to ten rounds per magazine. I reviewed 10 pistols. Ten pistols x 30 rounds = 300 rounds! And, I am just a regular gun owner, not even a competitive shooter. It wouldn't be hard to imagine a competitive shooter going through a few thousand rounds per month.

Do you know how much space 1,000 rounds of 9mm ammo takes up? A box that's 14"x6"x6." Surprising isn't it? Think about that the next time you hear a news report that police found thousands of rounds of ammo in a home. Was it two thousand? That's about two shoeboxes worth of ammunition.

Also, think about how the price of ammo fluctuates dramatically and why it may make sense to store ammo, just like people stored toilet paper during the 2020 Coronavirus pandemic. Is it smarter to buy more rounds than you need for immediate use when the price is $.27/round, or only buy what you need that day and spend $.89/round at another time?

It's not illegal to own thousands of rounds of ammunition.

And how about silencers/suppressors? The media makes being in possession of one of these seem like a criminal act, but in 42 states, you don't need a permit to own a silencer. The purchase is regulated by the NFA, and you do have to pay an additional tax.

You may be asking why in the world you'd want a silencer? Aren't those for snuffing out guys in those spy movies? If you're not doing something illegal, why would you want a silencer?

I can think of a couple of reasons—first, if someone breaks into your home, you probably won't have the presence of mind nor time to put in your earplugs if you need to draw a firearm to protect yourself and your family. The sound of a firearm discharge can distract you from the threat at hand by causing ringing in your ears or temporary hearing loss. If you use a silencer you'll still have your hearing and focus. Second, it reduces the noise at the shooting range.

Whether naive or due to an agenda, reporters shape citizens' views of guns and gun owners.

Laws in your State

Our forefathers designed the Constitution in a way that gives power to states, so naturally, laws vary by state.

Laws in the gun world change quickly, and unless you are a regular on the online gun boards, some of them will fly under the radar. So make sure you always check the law in your state.

A recent example of a law changing came on March 3, 2020, when a law changed in Michigan regarding compliance with the Brady Law when transferring a firearm to an unlicensed person. Now, a valid Michigan Concealed Pistol License (CPL) is no longer an alternative to initiating the National Instant Criminal Background Check System (NICS) during the firearm transfer. Background checks must be conducted for everyone.

Licensed dealers were likely aware of the new law, but citizens could have been caught off-guard.

Always check with the ATF and your state's firearms laws to keep up-to-date on laws affecting you.

I am writing this from Arizona, the heart of the Wild West. A perfect place to write a book about women and guns. Here, gun laws are among the least restrictive of any of our states. Right next door, the state of California is among the most restrictive. Although the states are all bound to the Second Amendment—that's at the federal level—the individual state laws vary based on their interpretation of what it means to bear arms.

There are no federal requirements in Arizona that private sellers need to meet when they sell firearms, meaning that they don't have to run a background check, ask for identification, or have their customers fill out any forms. Does this surprise you?

Generally, you'll find that conservative states allow more freedoms around gun regulations than liberal states.

Conservative Arizona passed an "Arizona Constitutional Carry" law in 2010. Under this law, if you are legally able to own a firearm and you're 21 years old or older, you can conceal carry in Arizona without a concealed weapon permit. However, you still must abide by all concealed-carry laws and off-limit signs.[14]

Arizona still issues carry permits that require a background check if you want such a permit, but again, it's not necessary.

There is no federal law requiring gun owners to be registered; however, some states require it.

There is no federal gun registry, so it's impossible to get an accurate number of guns owned in the US.

You need to know the laws in your state. Don't be afraid of the law. Know it and follow it.

Check out this example of one state's interpretation of the law.

In early 2020 at the panic of the coronavirus outbreak Champaign, Illinois, Mayor Deborah Frank Feinen signed an executive order declaring a state of emergency for the city.

"Among the powers Feinen gained after signing the executive order was the power to ban the sale of guns, ammunition, alcohol, and gasoline," according to a March 13 article in the Washington Examiner.

Can you see why it's important to know the laws of your own state?

TRANSPORTING IN YOUR CAR

In most states, firearms may be transported legally if they are unloaded, cased, and locked in the automobile trunk or otherwise inaccessible to the driver or any passenger. Know the law in your state and any states you are travelling to or through.

GUN LAWS AND MASS SHOOTINGS

Nearly half of adults (47 percent) say there would be fewer mass shootings if it were harder for people to obtain guns legally, according to a 2018 Pew Research study.[15]

Can I be real here with you? I get angry when people call for more gun control laws, but not for the reasons you may think. For me, regarding preventing mass shootings, further gun restrictions are the lazy man's solution. It's not getting at the heart of the issue at the cause in most mass shootings.

In the *Los Angeles Times*, they reported the findings from a study done by the Violence Project funded by the research arm of the US Department of Justice. "The vast majority of mass shooters in our study experienced early childhood trauma and exposure to violence at a young age. The nature of their exposure included parental suicide, physical or sexual abuse, neglect, domestic violence, and/or severe bullying. The trauma was often a precursor to mental health concerns, including depression, anxiety, thought disorders or suicidality."[16] And nearly every mass shooter had reached an "identifiable crisis point" leading up to the shooting.

Rather than believing in the false fence created by more laws, I'd like to see us be proactive and invest in our children by aggressively addressing and treating the mental health of our young people.

Insurance/Legal Protection

You're doing your research and wonder if you need insurance when you get a gun. It's a good question. After all, what if you're involved in a firearms incident, who ya gonna call? When you say *insurance* what you're really looking for is legal protection. While it isn't necessary, it is highly recommended especially for people who conceal carry.

This type of insurance or legal protection is commonly called CCW insurance. CCW stands for Carrying a Concealed Weapon. The goal of this *insurance* is to legally protect and defend yourself in a firearms incident, and you have a couple of options: have a good attorney on speed-dial or get legal protection membership.

A good attorney is one who answers the phone at 2 a.m. to give you legal counsel after you've had an altercation with a firearm, and one who specializes in firearms law. It's always good to get referrals, but if you are new to the gun world and don't know someone yet who could recommend an attorney, then you still have the second option, which is to get insurance.

Do you need insurance? Although it's not required, here's why you may want it.

If a thug breaks into your home and you shoot him in self-defense, you're in the clear, right? Not so fast. In this sue-crazy society, the victim or even the victim's family may come after you in civil court. Yes, even though your house was locked, the person broke in, and you shot him, you can still be in for a court battle.

Crazy isn't it?

WHAT TO LOOK FOR IN A CCW INSURANCE PLAN

Attorney fees

It makes sense that this part will cost you the most, and it's the part where you need to read the fine print when comparing plans. If the incident goes to trial, you could face hundreds of thousands of dollars in legal fees. Without a good policy, you may be forced to sell your home or other assets for your legal defense. Look at the policy's caps.

Bail bond fee

If you are a law-abiding citizen, the only time you used the word bail bond in a sentence is when you were talking about Duane the Dog Bounty hunter. The goal of having our bail bond fee covered is to reduce the time spent in jail so you can care for your kids, continue to earn a living, and help in your self-defense.

Coverage across state lines

You already learned that gun laws vary from state to state, so it shouldn't be a surprise that every insurance provider does not cover every state. If you plan on taking your gun with you when you travel across state lines, pay attention to this. If you are only using the gun for protection within your home, then this coverage isn't going to sway your decision.

Spousal coverage

If you have a spouse, check for discounted spousal add-on costs.

Although you may be a newbie to shooting and not sure if you want a gun of your own, if you are in house with a gun, it's possible you could be in a bad situation wishing you had coverage.

Imagine that thug breaks in, your brave husband goes to confront him, but in a struggle, the gun is knocked from hubby's hands and you pick it up (because you're brave too), and shoot the intruder in self-defense. Is your spouse's protection going to protect you? The time to answer that question is before any incident occurs.

If your spouse has insurance and you're not on it, why not? Talk to them today about adding you to it.

Education

Some of the providers offer education and legal information to members. Some offer CCW training.

CONCEALED-CARRY INSURANCE/ LEGAL PROTECTION PROVIDERS

United States Concealed Carry Association (USCCA)
Armed Citizens Legal Defense Network (ACLDN)
U.S. Law Shield
CCW Safe
Second Call Defense
Firearms Legal Protection
Legal Shield

Plans start at a range from $11–$50 per month.

There's an excellent insurance comparison chart on the Legal Shield website. Start there.

CHAPTER 6

FINDING THE RIGHT HANDGUN FOR YOU

The day the gun club called to tell me I cleared the background check and that my gun—my very first gun—came in was the same day I learned my partner cheated on me! Oh boy, I thought as I went to pick up my pistol. This does not look good.

I bought it anyway.

I was a late bloomer. Got my first one at age 37. And never shot it. Buying something and never using it? That is all kinds of wrong. When I go clothes shopping and bring in my bag from the car, I head straight for the bedroom and dump my loot on the bed. Then, even though I tried all the items on in the dressing room, I try them on again! You know, because they may look different in different lighting, and now I can try them on with different shoes and stuff. Come on, tell me I'm not alone?!

Buying a gun and letting it sit in the case is the equivalent of shopping, hanging up new clothes with tags in my closet, and *never* wearing them. Stupid and a waste of money. So why would I do that with my very first gun?

Let me tell you why. It wasn't a gun I wanted; it was the gun my instructor chose for me.

You need to choose your own gun. The gun that's right for you includes many things that should be factored into your purchase.

There are two common types of handguns—a revolver and a semi-automatic. Did the voice in your head just say "danger, danger" when you heard semi-automatic? Aren't those more dangerous? Think back to what you read about news reporting.

Not necessarily. The majority of handguns I see at the range are semi-automatics; otherwise, known as pistols. And if you were being taught by your boyfriend or husband who was in any type of armed services, they won't even show you a revolver. You would think being in the west, I would see more revolvers; after all, back in the day revolvers were as common as cacti. Besides the nostalgia of the old west, there are other things people like about revolvers.

When I was in my mid-twenties, a guy friend of mine took me to a shooting range to shoot his revolver. We were in the end lane. He shot first and then asked me to step to the line. I was terrified! I couldn't even hold the gun! So, he shot again and then asked me to step to the line. That time I held it up but set it back down again. Then he asked me to pick it up again and aim. I did, but was scared as hell! This was a big gun and I had never shot before! He got behind me and pulled the trigger as I held the gun. DO NOT DO THIS! Not the safest thing to do. Finally, I picked up the gun, aimed, set it down, picked it up, aimed, and pulled the trigger. Wow! I felt powerful at that moment.

Is a revolver or a handgun going to be your gun of choice?

Revolver vs Semi-automatic

There are advantages to both kinds of handguns and you need to weigh those along with all factors on the checklist I built for you—more on that in the next chapter.

For now, let's have a little fun with this! If there were a handgun dating app that compared the revolver or the semi-automatic pistol, when would you swipe right? (In dating apps, a swipe right means you're interested.)

REVOLVERS AND SIGNS YOU'D SWIPE RIGHT

First, you aren't into complicated relationships; revolver mechanics are simple—it has fewer moving parts, which means less can go wrong.

Second, you can go a full day without taking a shower and be OK with that. You don't need to be a fanatic about revolver hygiene since you have fewer parts to clean. If cleaning isn't your thing, this may just be your match.

Third, you avoid confrontation. If you are just learning to shoot, you may like a revolver because there's less sass. A revolver has less recoil so you don't have to fight it.

Fourth, you'll drive around for five minutes looking for the least expensive gas. Revolvers are less expensive, which means you could get a revolver *and* afford premium ammo. Bonus!

Finally, you don't play any racquet sports and arm curls make you cringe. You need to consider your strength and biology when you're choosing the right gun for you. Since a revolver doesn't have a slide to rack, it doesn't require as much strength. (Racking the slide refers to pulling the slide back in order to empty an empty cartridge in the chamber.) If you know you have weak hands and forearms, you've had surgery or arthritis, or are missing a finger, a revolver may be your gun of choice. However, you must have a strong trigger finger because the trigger on the revolvers is more resistant than on a pistol.

How are you feeling? Do you have a pitter-patter in your heart for revolvers? Is your finger itching to swipe right? I mean, what's not too like?

The first time I shot, it was with a revolver.

My first time was with a revolver; nevertheless, I never swiped right. I read the profile, asked around about it, tried it a few times, but we weren't a match. In fact, I never went back to the revolver except to test some for you. If you love revolvers, we will never fight over the same gun. This could be the start of a beautiful friendship.

Instead, I swiped right on the semi-automatic pistol.

SEMI-AUTOMATICS AND SIGNS YOU'D SWIPE RIGHT

First, you like efficiency. A pistol has the potential to carry more rounds. I use a 15-round magazine when I am target shooting because the higher capacity decreases the time I take reloading. And less time reloading means more time shooting.

Second, you like laid back. The trigger resistance on a pistol is typically less than that on a revolver. It's like a ballet versus a mosh pit.

Third, you like a slimmer profile. A pistol has a slimmer side view than a revolver. If you are going to concealed carry, I recommend a semi-automatic.

Finally, you shower regularly. Semi-automatics do better when cleaned regularly to decrease the chance of a malfunction. If you don't like to clean, maybe a revolver is your gun of choice.

I determined early on that a semi-automatic was my handgun of choice.

Will it be yours?

Whichever type of handgun you choose, the most important thing is to get comfortable with it and learn to shoot it accurately. And remember, there isn't a right gun, only the right gun for you.

How to Choose the Right Gun

So now you know whether you want a revolver or semi-automatic. But there are several types of revolvers and semi-automatics. To pick which one is right for you, you need to go through a few tests.

HAND DOMINANCE TEST

Feeling LEFT out? My mom is a lefty. I grew up wondering why I couldn't cut anything with her scissors. I never realized how bad lefties have it until I started shooting.

Most guns are designed for those with right-hand dominance, although a few guns are made for lefties. Cabot Guns is a niche manufacturer of left-handed 1911s. While you're searching for the right gun for you, be sure to notice if it has left-handed features.

You should eventually be able to shoot a gun one-handed if needed. You'll want to try this with your dominant hand. This takes some practice and strength so don't be discouraged if you aren't able to do it at first. Once you feel comfortable doing it one-handed, then you have passed this test.

EYE DOMINANCE TEST

Did you know most people have a dominant eye? Even subtle differences can affect your shooting accuracy.

You can do a rough test of this right now. Hold your hand out in front of you. Close one eye, and align your hand, still stretched out so your index finger is in front of your nose. With your eye still closed, tell me which one is open? Your eye that remained opened is likely your dominant eye. We go through life favoring one eye over the other. When you look through a telescope, which eye do you use? Another clue to your eye dominance.

Want to be really sure?

Create an isosceles triangle (nod to you geometry nerds) with your hands by joining your index fingers and thumbs. Your index fingers form the top point of the triangle and your thumbs will overlap. Got it? Okay, now with both eyes look at a fixed object at least 10 feet away. Holding your hand triangle directly in front of you, position the object in the middle of the triangle. Close your left eye and leave your right eye open—if the item stays centered, you are right-eye dominant. Similarly, close your right eye and leave your left eye open, and if the item stays centered, you are left-eye dominant.

If you are right-handed but left-eye dominant, or left-handed but right-eye dominant, it's called cross-eye dominant.

I'm cross-eye dominant because I'm left-eye dominant but right-handed. However, the only time it's been an issue for me is when I shoot a rifle due to the ergonomics and position of the sight.

Why does it matter?

I told you what tight groupings are and that you could learn a lot about your shooting from your groupings. I am left-eye dominant, so when I shoot, I tend to be to the left of center. When I am low on the target, I blame my height, but really that's not what's causing it. Sure, it's a factor, but it has more to do with needing to adjust my position slightly. If you have a tight grouping, but it's not where you wanted it to be, look at it. It's like reading tea leaves. Shoot and adjust, shoot and adjust.

PICKING A HANDGUN TO FIT YOU GRIP

The size of your hand and your grip strength are important factors when deciding on the right gun for you. If you aren't holding your gun properly, it may slip from your hands, or you will lose precision if you can't hold it steady. You may also feel it dig into your hand or your hand may cramp. Plus, it's just not fun to shoot a gun that's not the right gun for you!

Measure your hand size and grip to get your grip diameter and then compare that to the grip sizes on the handguns you test.

Hand size

A person's hand size is measured by the length of their hand. The average hand size for males is 7.44" and the average size for females is 6.77."

To figure out the length of your hand, measure the distance from the fold in your wrist below the palm to the tip of your middle finger when your hand is flat. You'll need this number for the next step.

It's probably no surprise to you that guns are frequently designed for the "average male" hand.

Grip diameter

Measure your hand's grip diameter and use it to calculate your grip size. As a rule, 20 percent of your hand length equals your grip diameter.[17]

Or you can use the "OK" test.

Make the okay sign using your thumb and index finger and then measure the inside of the "O" formed to find the diameter.

That is your grip diameter.

Now calculate your grip size by multiplying your grip diameter by 3.14. You may recognize this from your geometry days as pi, the ratio of the circumference of any circle to the diameter of that circle.

You can start with this basic grip measurement as a guide, but know that there are after-market grips that can be added your handgun to improve the grip-ability of your gun either due to the texture or the few millimeters of added circumference.

Tip: If you want to be a better shooter, improve your grip strength.

SHOOTING STANCE

I've noticed when women get in a shooting stance, we tend to lean back and away from the handgun and from the target. This isn't a stable, empowered position, and if you're shooting a gun with a lot of recoil, it could knock you off-balance.

We do this because subconsciously we want to move away. We are apprehensive. It's natural when we are uncertain of something or someone to lean back. That's basic body language. Next time you talk with someone, notice how they are leaning. Is it toward you, or away from you? When you like someone, you tend to lean in closer to hear what they're saying.

You want to lean into the target, like it's a date that intrigues you. Act very interested in the target, not fearful. You want to get to know the target better.

How we move and position our body influences how we feel.

Besides the psychological changes you feel, by slightly leaning toward the target, you will be better prepared for any recoil.

Here's another exercise to try with a friend, to show you what a difference it makes. Stand up straight, hips facing forward. Ask your friend to stand in front of you and to push lightly on your shoulders while you try to resist. Next, lean slightly forward and ask your friend to do the same thing. Do you feel the difference? You have greater resistance because you are using the weight of your body, leaning forward, and your muscles are already engaged and ready to resist.

You're leaning into the energy.

Try this exercise. Stand up and raise your hands above you in a V shape and say, "I am powerful. I am strong. I am confident." Then lower them and repeat it three times. How do you feel? Pretty good right? It works, doesn't it? If you didn't do the exercise, ask yourself is that how you're going through life? Observing? Or do you want to take charge of your life and your circumstances? This is it! Time to step into who you are. Your past does not equal your present. You are a woman—brave, intuitive, and wonderfully made. Let's see the V! You can do this!

Checklist

The first impression of a gun isn't like the first impression of a person. All of us, either consciously or subconsciously, gather data about a person when we first meet them. Their appearance, manners, mannerisms, and voice all come into play. And within 10 seconds, we formulate an initial impression.

However, with guns, first impressions aren't reliable because guns are full of surprises as you'll see in one of my reviews in the next chapter. When you're testing a gun for purchase, you could become overwhelmed and forget what you liked about one gun over the other. You need a system to keep track of your likes and dislikes.

I compare it to the way we shop for clothing.

We can have 20 different blouse-and-pant combos in a fitting room, but we keep track of how much we like or dislike them by asking questions from this unwritten checklist we've crafted and revised over years of shopping experience and changing body shapes. Does this make my butt look fat? How many times will I wear it? Is it worth the cost? Will I need to buy additional accessories to make this outfit work?

I love fitting rooms that have three hooks because I can use my system. I start by putting everything on the first hook. When I try on something and it's a definite no, I move it to the second hook. If it's okay and I want to compare it to others, I move it to the third hook. After I've tried everything on, I go back to the third hook and go through the process again to narrow it down.

You don't need a checklist to track your likes when you go clothes shopping because you've done this a million times and you know what you're doing. Women's minds are amazing!

While your fitting room testing may last hours, your gun testing may span weeks, depending on your ability to get your hands on the gun you want to test. You need a process of elimination when shopping for a gun too, but it will need to be different since you can't sort your guns on hooks! Don't rely on your memory. You need a checklist!

I developed a gun checklist that's available for you today on my website. I included key points you need to rate in your evaluation such as recoil, caliber, size, and even your feelings. Download a copy of the checklist for each gun you review.

Balance your purpose for the gun with your rankings.

Remember, I loved how I felt shooting the 1911, but it wasn't my gun of choice because it didn't match my purpose of concealed carry.

If you're a little skittish about shooting and have the opportunity to shoot more than one caliber, I recommend starting with the smallest caliber—the .22. The weight and balance of this sized pistol inspire confidence and peace of mind that you have things under control.

You don't have to make a decision right away because you can rent guns at the range. The cost is minimal and well worth trying before buying. You can even hire an instructor to show you the pros and cons of each of the guns as you shoot them. Don't be afraid to try a bunch to narrow your selection.

Ladies, besides all the test-firing and researching you do before buying your gun, notice how you feel. When you hold the gun, do you feel empowered, confident? Women have this gift of intuition and we need to use it more often. Shooting seems like such a left-brain activity that you may think you need to stuff the feeling part of you. I say screw that. Embrace the feeling part of you! When you are shooting a gun for the first time how do you *feel*?

In the next chapter, I evaluate some handguns for you. So come on, girls, let's go shopping!

Download the checklist at the website, handgunsforher.com and use one per gun. Then, take a photo of the gun and a photo of your rankings sheet right after it so the photos are sequential. It makes it so much easier to keep track of your rankings.

CHAPTER 7

HANDGUN REVIEWS

I reviewed a few handguns for you to show the variety that's out there, and to show you the importance of taking notes as you test each one so you can determine if it's the right gun for you.

All the pistols were from the factory, meaning none had after-market accessories such as custom grips or sights.

For each of the guns, I shot three magazines. That gave me a enough repetition to rate accuracy, the slide, reload, and recoil. Prices are from Summer 2020, and are meant to be a comparison point—please do your own price shopping before your final decision.

As you rank each gun using the checklist I provided, remember why you want a gun—whether it's protection, recreation, or competition.

☑ MY GUN CHOICE CHECKLIST

MAKE/MODEL/CALIBER: _____

	BAD	OKAY	GOOD	GREAT	LOVE IT!
	1	2	3	4	5
RECOIL					
EASY SLIDE					
RELOAD					
SAFETY					
CONFIDENCE					
ERGONOMICS					
ACCURACY					
SIZE FOR PURPOSE					
SUITS MY PURPOSE					
OVERALL FEELING					
COST					
TOTAL					

Downloadable from handgunsforher.com.

Walther PP22Q

Caliber: .22LR
Cost: $300

Right away, I thought, this doesn't look like a twenty-two caliber—.22s are small, but this wasn't.

The slide was smooth and easy. The recoil was minimal and reloading was so easy.

It doesn't have a traditional safety, meaning there's not an external lever that you flip to stop it from firing.

The grip was ridged but too big to feel comfortable in my hand.

After shooting this, I realized I needed a column in my checklist for "accuracy" because I was dead on with this one since it's a very submissive gun—the ease of the slide, the reload, and its light feel made me feel like I was in control of this thing. This is a perfect gun for newbies.

You don't have to fight it, its small caliber doesn't pack a kick, and it's quiet. Quiet as guns go. I recommend this for you if you have a lot of fear built up around shooting.

Lesson: Start with a smaller caliber if you need time to get used to the sound and recoil of other calibers.

Firearms manufacturer Walther Arms, Inc. is known for the P38 9mm pistol used by the Germans in WW2.

In 2012 a new subsidiary, Walther Arms, Inc, launched the 22LR.

The PPQ has what are commonly referred to as *Glock Features*, making it a favorite of many shooters. *Glock Features* commonly refers to the trigger mechanism, specifically that the trigger is the safety. The phrase implies there's no external safety, uses a US-style magazine button release, and has minimal total parts in the firearms. Fewer parts generally lead to a more reliable product.

The PPQ chambered in 22LR is possibly the most reliable and easy to shoot 22LR pistol.

The Walther PPQ in 22LR is also the easiest of the semi-automatic pistols to chamber a live round via manipulating the slide of the firearm. Since the 22LR round has lower delivered energy, the recoil spring of the pistol is "lighter" than larger calibers. The pistol slide is also lighter in weight on 22LR pistols.

The lower weight of the slide combined with the lighter recoil spring allows the pistol to be cocked back and loaded easier than a steel slide and a heavier recoil spring. This is a huge benefit for shooters that have difficulty with grasping the slide to chamber a live round.

The Walter PPQ in 22LR is the pistol I recommend to shooters with low hand strength, nerve damage to the hand, arthritis, and even prosthetics. Along with all its great features, it is just a fun gun to shoot.

Twenty-two Caliber 1911

Caliber: .22LR
Cost: $550

I didn't know the 1911 came in a .22 until a few years after I started shooting. I shot the 1911 .45 many times before. Not gonna lie here, I was excited to shoot this!

The first thing I noticed was how cold it was when I picked it up! Cold metal, not polymer like those last ones.

The magazine release was awkward for me, maybe because my hand was too small and I really had to reposition to punch it with my thumb. A thing about mag releases—most are for right-handed people so are on the left side—seems counterintuitive writing it—but the reason for this is you release the magazine with your thumb. Since your right hand is holding the gun, your right hand will release the magazine. Other than that, it felt comfortable in my hand. It has a beavertail hand rest, which took some of the weight off my forearm. Ergonomically, this was a 10! Although, on my rating system, the highest rating is a 4.

It has a standard safety and a secondary safety on the grip.

Shooting it was a dream. It seemed to want to hit the bullseye. I could have shot this for hours, but I had five more guns to review.

The 1911 .22 has the intimidating look of a classic 1911, but it didn't behave like the beast that the 1911, .45 is.

SIG Sauer Mosquito

Caliber: .22LR
Cost: Discontinued. Used cost varies.

Next, the SIG Mosquito. If I could have dropped this in the trash on my way out, I would have been fine with that. It was like a date that starts out promising, and then you find out he lives with his mom, picks his teeth with his dirty fingers, and can't linger over dinner because he is on "work release."

The SIG Mosquito was discontinued. I hesitated to include this review, but I want you to learn from my experience. Not everything in the gun world is perfect.

Here's what happened. First, it started off well and I had high hopes. It had a mild recoil, an easy slide, and reloading was super simple. It does have a safety, for those of you who want that feature. It fit my hand nicely—and my hand is small. For most of you, this matters and you should search for a gun that fits. The grip was smooth.

Initially, I thought, I'd probably rank this one quite high overall.

And then, shit hit the fan.

So there I was, on my second magazine, noticing how comfortable the SIG felt in my hands. But it jammed twice. Once per magazine, I had to stop and drop the round. If you shoot for even a short time, you will probably experience a jam. Most are mild. What happens is that the bullet doesn't get pushed all the way through the chamber and catches on something. All you have to do is tilt the gun sideways, pull back on the slide, and the bullet easily

106

drops out. You can just let it drop. Don't worry about where it goes; just forget about it and move on. It's not going to explode, and it's not going to fire on its own.

Usually, it is that easy. Pull the slide. This is another important reason that you need a gun with a slide that you can pull back.

But after the second jam, I was annoyed. This was distracting and I was trying to be extra focused so I could be detailed about my feedback for you. I was prepared to go through all three magazines though, to be consistent.

But that didn't happen.

I returned to my shooting stance after clearing the chamber and fired. Suddenly something didn't feel right. The gun felt loose. It took me a second to understand what I was seeing when I looked at the gun.

The entire left side had sheared off! I could see inside the gun! It was like transformers where you see the side of the face. And this gun was terminated! I was stunned.

The range master knew something bad had happened, so he approached. He'd never seen anything like that. If I would have been a newbie, I would have left the range and called it a day.

No one wants to think about a gun falling apart in your hands, but as long as no one gets hurt, don't freak out.

.380 Colt Mustang

Caliber: .380
Cost: $530

This is a super small gun! Normally the smaller the gun, the more the recoil, but I found the kick on this to be reasonable and not overpowering. I gave it a five on recoil.

There was a long trigger pull and I think that's what lead to my horrible accuracy. Or at least that is the story I told myself.

This is when it pays to know what kind of shooter you are. I know if I think too much about what I'm firing at, I get all up in my head and I am focusing too much about the shot instead of just taking it. It seems counterintuitive, but that's what I know about my shooting style. That trigger pull was long enough to throw me off. Also, because you need to apply extra pressure to the trigger, you'll need a strong trigger finger for this gun.

There was some unexpected resistance with the slide and it doesn't have a safety.

I also had problems getting the magazine in—I had to push hard on it to get it to click into place. In fact, I thought it was in and I went to shoot and it slid out about a centimeter. It seemed gummy to me. I'd never had that happen and maybe because it only holds six rounds it was light and I probably thought I didn't need to use as much force.

Given all these factors, I gave it a rank of one for the ergonomics category.

Springfield Armory Hellcat

Caliber: 9mm
Cost: $569

This is called a micro-compact gun, and size makes it a good design for concealed carry, so for purpose for me, it ranked a five.

I felt a lot of resistance with the slide and I gave it a rank of two for that. Recoil also got a two. The barrel is short, so you will get more kick with this 9mm. The longer the barrel the less kick.

This is where you consider whether the kick is a fair trade-off for the size. I can't emphasize this enough—download my gun choice checklist from my website and use it while you're testing guns!

I gave it a one for "Accuracy." Some guns you click with and some you don't. I adjusted the tilt, grip, and distance of the target just so I could hit a bullseye, but it never happened. I may compromise on a bigger kick for a smaller size, but I will never compromise on accuracy.

The Hellcat has a huge capacity for its size—12 rounds standard. Generally in any shooting situation the more shots available before reloading, the better.

Compare this to the Sig P365 also reviewed here.

Colt 1911

Caliber: 9mm
Cost: $1,199

If you have weak hands, this could be the gun for you! The slide is super easy to pull—so easy it's noticeable compared to any gun I've ever shot.

This is a good gun to train with. The slide is so smooth that it will be easier to rack to clear jams and you'll feel more in control rather than fighting the gun. It's a 9mm too so the kick isn't bad, in fact I ranked it a five.

If considering this 1911 for home use, it would have scored a five in seven of the categories. However, when I considered my purpose to be concealed carry, I scored this gun fives in only five of the categories. I gave it a rank of one for "Suits my purpose." This is where it becomes evident that when you factor in the purpose of the gun—and you absolutely must—it influences the overall ranking.

As much as I gush about this gun, there are a couple of drawbacks. First, the capacity is only seven. Second, it has a beavertail, and because of the risk of it catching on something in a purse or bag, I'd leave this one at home, since there are so many better options for concealed carry. Third, for me, it's a bit long for a concealed carry. Side note, there is a shorter version of this gun that's called an Officer's Model.

If you're looking for a gun for protection at home, I recommend this 1911.

Glock 43 Subcompact

Caliber: 9mm
Cost: $530

If you don't want to mess with anything finicky, this could be the gun for you. Also, Glocks are reliable and used by military and police.

The main differentiator here is how this Glock holds its ammo.

Most Glocks are what's called *double stacked*—this means that the ammunition sits two-by-two in the magazine, rather than single stacked in single file. The Glock 43 is single stacked.

This simple design tweak gives this Glock a slim profile and makes it a good choice as a concealed carry firearm.

The drawback is that because it's only single stacked, it holds less ammo—only six in the mag, and one in the chamber. That's not a lot.

Other points: no external safety, it has features lefties, and it has a good kick.

Plus, there are a lot of after-market add on options.

Not fun to shoot.

I also tried the Glock 43X after this one. It's larger than the 43 and has a larger capacity of 10 rounds because it's double-stacked.

Springfield XD-S

Caliber: 9mm
Cost: $400

When this first came on the market I had to try it, I loved its look, but I was disappointed.

It has a rough grip and a stubborn slide, and the trigger reach is too long for my finger and it only holds seven rounds. Darn it.

The top reason I was disappointed in this Springfield was that my accuracy was horrible.

Jeff was with me when I tested this one and happened to have a laser. The laser spotlights whatever your gun is pointing at—it's like a laser you'd use in a presentation, but way more powerful. There's no mistaking where the gun is pointed. This is a good training tool and I think Jeff was hoping my aim would improve with it. It improved somewhat, but not enough for me to be confident with this gun. It got a one on my checklist for accuracy.

Remember, just because I don't rank it highly, doesn't mean it's a gun you shouldn't try. The point with using a ranking sheet is that you can track and rank the different categories, and then decide for yourself.

When that man in your life steers you to the gun that's right for him, it may not be right for you when you factor in your rankings. If you go to him with a ranking sheet, you also have a solid reason not to choose a gun, instead of only saying you didn't like it. This piece of advice when used wisely may just save your relationship!

SIG P365

Caliber: 9mm
Cost: $450

I have so many good things to say about this gun. The first thing I noticed on this one was the size. It is noticeably small, even for a concealed carry gun. In fact, SIG Sauer classifies the SIG P365 as a micro-compact.

The grip on this was smooth. Like freshly shaven skin—you notice it. The smooth surface makes it a good choice for carrying in your purse because it reduces the chance of it getting caught on anything. Also, there's no external safety.

This was a loud gun with lots of recoil. Because of the recoil, I opted not to shoot three magazines with this one as it hurt my hand, my thumb especially. Shoot several rounds with each gun to give you enough time to notice any areas where you are sore. Then determine if it's due to an injury or weakness, or if the discomfort is due to something inherent in the gun.

The real bonus in this one is that it can hold 10 rounds in the magazine and 1 in the chamber. This is an outstanding feature.

Even though the kick was too much for my thumb, I still highly recommend this one for someone with small hands.

It's a solid choice—ranked the 2020 #1 choice in concealed carry handguns for women by *Gun Digest*. And as a bonus, it is easy to clean.

Colt Para 1911

Caliber: .45
Cost: $1,100

It has a sleek look, black and silver—that was my first impression. I picked it up and noticed the cold, very cold metal.

This .45 had a classic rough recoil. A good stance is important when shooting this one, so you don't get knocked on your ass. (Another reason why wearing heels while shooting is a bad idea at first; You'll be thrown off-balance.)

The slide was easy to move but was only moderately easy to reload and I ranked it three for that.

It has a dual safety—the external lever and the one on the handle.

I had a 3.5 confidence level shooting the 1911 Para. I liked the ergonomics and my overall feeling, but its punch is more powerful than what I want.

The trigger on this was straight instead of curved like other guns I reviewed.

The gun has an alligator grip; this thing left imprints in my hand after two magazines! The alligator ridges are hard and deep to help you hold the gun.

As with all 1911s, I had high accuracy with this. Does everyone shoot well with this? It made me wonder if it was the design, the shooter, or that the design was right for the shooter.

Smith & Wesson 1911

Caliber: .45
Cost: $1,150

The first time I shot the 1911, boy, was it intimidating. From the profile to the caliber to the sound to the recoil, this is not a gun to be messed with.

In full disclosure, I have shot the 1911 many times, and it is my favorite gun to shoot. Read on to find out why I never purchased one—and it has nothing to do with the cost.

The recoil on this thing is tremendous. No way could I shoot more than one round one-handed—it would jump right out of my hand! The sound is noticeably louder than those .22s I reviewed. There's no mistaking this is a .45 caliber. I ranked it one for recoil.

The slide is not for those with weak upper bodies. It takes some pulling power here. To prepare for shooting this gun, you might need to do some finger pushups, forearm lifts, or maybe try a rowing machine. The reload is hard for me too and kind of awkward because the grip is too large for my hand. It has a thin profile.

However, it has a beavertail, which helps the gun feel very balanced in my hand. A beavertail is at the top of the handle of some guns and is like a ledge that your hand bumps or rests underneath. And, well, it looks like a beavertail. Interestingly, I felt my left bicep was getting a workout! This gun called upon my strength in both arms to safely hold it. A cool thing about the 1911 is you could shoot it left-handed.

When I shoot this, I feel powerful and confident. And I am crazy accurate. Then, why haven't I purchased a 1911?

In a defensive situation, I am concerned I would not have the time nor would I have the chance to get in the right stance and be able to put two hands on it. I really have to lean into the target to face the recoil. I am not comfortable enough with this one—yet—to take it to the range alone. I like the security of having an instructor or another person who shoots 1911s regularly with me when I shoot this one.

While it can be good for protection at home, it's not practical for concealed carry, so I ranked it a one for my purpose.

Lesson here: Know your limitations and be honest about them.

CHAPTER 8

CHOOSING THE RIGHT AMMO

One of the most daunting things, when I started looking for my forever gun, was which ammunition I should buy. You may remember one of the fears I went over in an earlier chapter—fear of loading the wrong ammunition into a gun. Caliber, grain, it was like a spaghetti bowl of confusion. Don't worry, I'll explain that next.

There are different calibers, or sizes, of ammunition. If you have any propensity toward math or physics, you are going to like this part. I don't, so this is painful for me. You owe me; I'm taking one for the gun sisterhood.

Caliber

Caliber describes the bullet diameter. And each handgun is designed to use only one caliber.

Let's start with the basics.

COMMON HANDGUN CALIBERS

Think of common caliber types for handguns as small, medium, and large. The small is the .22, the medium is the 9mm, and the large is the 45mm. That kind of makes sense, right, because the smaller the number, the smaller the caliber. The larger the caliber, the greater the stopping power.

.22 LR: Better than a knife for self-protection. Problem is it doesn't have great stopping power. Note—you can use this exact ammo in a handgun and a .22 hunting rifle. The .22 ammo is the most popular round on the market today.

.380 auto: Smallest most widely accepted caliber for sufficient protection (terminal effects).

9mm Luger: The most popular pistol caliber in the world. You can drop the "Luger" when referring to it for handgun use.

40 SW: The 40 Smith and Wesson is literally the compromise between the 9mm and the 45ACP. Used extensively in competition shooting and gaining for personal protection.

45 ACP: This is a big bold caliber that means business. This is like the Terminator of handgun calibers.

Rimfire and Centerfire

I'd put this in the FYI category. Tuck it away and when you hear it again, which may be a long time from now, it will sound familiar.

Rimfire and centerfire are two distinctions in the way ammo is manufactured. The rimfire's primer is built into the rim while the centerfire cartridge has the primer in the center. If you look at the flat bottom end of the cartridge and see a circle in the middle, that's a centerfire cartridge. A 9mm is a centerfire while a .22 is a rimfire. The only reason I can see why a beginner shooter needs to know this is that it factors into your overall gun cost—rimfires are way less expensive.

The One Grain You Shouldn't Eat

When you look at a box of ammunition, you'll see "gr" on it. Ammunition is measured in a unit of mass called grains (abbreviated "gr."). Usually, the heavier the bullet weight, the lower the velocity, while the lighter the bullet, the higher the velocity. Bullet grain varies based on caliber and manufacturer guidelines. As a beginner, don't lose sleep over this.

Velocity

We also need to talk about velocity. Let me put on my professor cap for a minute. And here it is . . . drumroll . . . Velocity is the speed at which something moves in one direction from a starting point. We measure velocity to determine how quickly the bullet will arrive at the target when fired from your gun. Whew. Okay, back to normal me. Oh wait, how about a quiz question. Q: At which point is the velocity of the bullet the greatest? From initial fire or when it reaches the target? Tick tock. Tick tock. A: At the beginning during the initial fire when it leaves the muzzle. There you go, your next bar trivia. You're welcome.

You can always ask the staff at the gun shop or shooting range about the intricacies of the caliber, brand, and grain. When in doubt for personal protection, choose ammo with the higher (faster) velocity. The rule of thumb is, velocity kills.

Cost and Availability

We go from discussing physics to economics. A philosophical question to ask is if you were to choose your caliber before your handgun, which would be best? Consider price and availability.

The cost and availability of ammo (and guns) are influenced by supply and demand big time. You think the stock market was volatile in 2020? That was nothing compared to the cost of ammo. For example, prices for a 9mm round in 2020 varied from a few cents in January to over $1 or unavailable in June!

It's basic economics of supply and demand. We don't need a million-dollar study to determine the mood of the country. Just look at the price of ammo. Here's what I'm talking about.

In late spring 2020, there was a surge in gun purchases, and by June 2020, 9mm ammo was hard to come by. Some stores ran out of guns and ammo due to the overwhelming demand for both.

Why the surge and scarcity?

The surge was caused by general feelings of uncertainty and panic as the nation and world faced COVID-19, which was quickly deemed a pandemic by experts.

During the coronavirus pandemic, government officials were granted authority to close businesses that were not "essential," to stop the spread of the virus. Officials closed gun and ammo stores, labeling them as non-essential businesses, effectively shutting down Second Amendment rights.

One of those government officials was Democrat NJ Governor Phil Murphy who, on March 21, 2020 ordered the state police to enforce a mandatory shutdown of gun and ammo stores. About 10 days later after much pushback, he was forced to change his stance.

The surge continued in May of that year with the fuel of civil unrest that included looting and riots after protests began over the death of George Floyd while in the hands of Minneapolis police.

Then, the call for defunding the police continued to fuel the surge—how will you protect yourself if the police can't get to you?

I expect the demand for guns and ammo to continue after the 2020 fall elections. A surge occurred heading into the last presidential election too, but for entirely different reasons. In 2016, the increase in demand for ammo and guns was partly due to the fear that the Obama administration would implement measures that would restrict the purchase and ownership of guns.

You can see how demand for guns and ammo is somewhat predictable—whenever people fear for their safety, or their Second Amendment rights are threatened, the demand increases.

Returning to that philosophical question about which ammo is best, I think it's comparable to investment advice—diversify. If you can afford to get two guns of two different calibers, do it. If you have a gun that takes the most popular handgun caliber (9mm) and it's not available or costly, you have a second handgun that requires different ammo such as a .22 or a .45 and may be more available and less expensive.

Manufactured Versus Homemade

Millions of weapon aficionados make their own ammunition, commonly called reloading—I call it homemade. This is labor intensive since you have to first collect the brass (case) then construct each cartridge by hand. If you have time on your hands and want to learn, you can save a lot of money—I've heard 50 percent off of retail price per piece.

Which one should you use in your gun?

One of my worst experiences at the range was using this homemade ammo.

The problem is if it's not done correctly, it can cause jams and be unreliable. I started shooting my friend's gun with his reloads and soon every other shot jammed. With the next magazine, four shots in a row jammed, and that's when I said I'm out.

As a beginner shooter you probably don't know anyone who makes their own ammo. Buy manufactured.

Shooting is fun, but when you're continually clearing jams, it's no fun at all.

PART THREE

EQUIP

CHAPTER 9

WHERE TO BUY

When you're ready to buy a firearm, where should you go? You can buy from a trusted friend, a local business that sells guns, a well-known business online, or you can go through a gun broker.

If you are a first-time gun buyer, I recommend getting a new one from a licensed seller.

Compare your purchase to buying a car. If you buy a car you find on Craigslist, what do you really know about it? Oh, the Carfax report? OK, and if someone is less than honest, and they go to a shady repair shop, do you think Carfax has a clue about that? Nope. Also, when you are new, you don't know what to look for.

You'll know the basics of a firearm after reading this book, but you're not going to know the intricacies of a gun yet. How do you know it is a good buy and safe? And if something goes wrong, what recourse do you have? Are you going to knock on Mr. Craigslist's door and ask for your money back? Oh, what's that? You don't even know where his door is because you met in a parking lot because it was safer?

Yes, some private sellers that don't have licenses are legit and reputable. I know people who buy and sell privately and have never had a problem. You know why? They know each other or a friend connected them. Note: If you buy from a friend, the gun won't be registered in your name. There's nothing necessarily wrong with that, remember?

If you don't have any trusted gun seller connections, buy your gun from a sporting goods store, a local gun club, or a local licensed dealer.

CHAPTER 10

ACCESSORIZE

Ladies, you are going to love this. You don't have to wear camouflage to the gun range, but maybe if you want to, you can wear fashionable camo. And if you want to carry, you are in luck because you have a lot of cute handbags and backpacks to choose from.

In 2017, the NRA put together its first "concealed-carry fashion show" for women. Bringing fashion to the foreground! The show included bra holsters and other concealed carry solutions for the professional woman. How cool is that?

Women brought color to the gun world. Before we came along, everyone wore black, khakis, or traditional camouflage. (Who are they hiding from at the range anyway?!)

Now manufactures are designing for the everyday woman whether she's going out for a run, heading to the store, or watching her kid's game—women have choices!

Don't shrink back and blend in. You are female and we are taking the industry by storm! More women than ever before own guns!

Concealed Carry Gear

Concealed carry gear is anything you're using to conceal your gun in public.

Three traditional types of carry options:

Off-the-body Carry—handbags, backpacks
Outside the body—holster
Appendix—tucked in jeans

Nowadays we have even more choices for concealed carry gear. Gear includes purses, backpacks, holsters, leggings, and more.

Women have a hidden-in-plain-sight place to put their gun—in their purse (called off-the-body carry). It's a typical accessory so it doesn't draw attention.

You'll be happy to learn there are many very fashionable purse designs ranging from casual to dressy.

When choosing the right handbag for your weapon of choice, you can start by considering how well your gun fits in it and decide if you want a cross-body design or an over-the-shoulder one.

Once you've made those decisions, practice reaching in and pretending to pull out your weapon. Can you access it easily and quickly? How many seconds does it take to get your gun out? When you place your gun in the purse, is it always in the same position? Is it secured in place so it doesn't jostle around? This is an important feature because you want consistency, leaving nothing to chance. If it comes with a built-in holster, does it meet your needs, or will you be purchasing another one? Ask the same questions for backpacks.

Once you purchase your new concealed carry bag, remember to position the bag the same way so you know which way your gun is pointing, allowing you to grab it quickly and easily every time.

Tip: One feature that's been added to some purses is a magnetic closure instead of a zipper in the gun pocket since it could take too long to get your gun out if you fumble with a zipper.

Handbags and backpacks aren't the only choices you have for concealed carry. Maybe you don't carry either now and that's fine; you have other options. You can get a holster or choose other clothing that's customized to hold small firearms.

Clothing

Alexo Athletics, run by CEO Amy Robbins, has a collection of activewear, including running tights, that have built-in carry compartments to hold your keys, your mace, your gun. Robbins founded Alexo Athletica in 2017, billing it as an athletic "carry wear" company for women who want to conceal guns on their person.

Holster

If you're jamming your gun in your purse, get a holster that covers the trigger. Like many women, we have a whole bunch of stuff in there: keys, baby wipes, makeup, phone, brush, toothbrush. In a threatening situation, you don't want to struggle with a mascara tube that's lodged behind the trigger. At home, you don't want to pull it and have something catch on it, causing the trigger to be pressed, with neighbors calling 911 to report shots fired.

Try this the next time you're in public: scan people's bodies and look in places where you'd put a gun—small of the back, pocket, between hip bone, and belly button—do you see an imprint of a gun?

Whatever accessory you get, evaluate its safety, quality, purpose, and comfort. And by all means, practice, practice, practice pulling out your gun so you're ready if you ever need to do it for real.

PART FOUR

EMPOWER

CHAPTER 11

TRAINING

Part of being a safe gun owner is to get the proper training in how to use your gun.

Shooting isn't like riding a bike. When you try to learn a bike, an adult comes alongside you to steady the bike while you pedal. After hours of this, they fool you by letting go and not telling you . . . and suddenly, without knowing it, you are riding your bike alone for the first time! Then, the next day you get up extra early and you ride your bike! You don't have to re-learn it from yesterday; you just know how to do it. And you're off to ride with your friends, down the block, completely solo. That's why they say it's as easy as riding a bike!

Shooting isn't like that. It's a perishable skill.

I have never heard someone say shooting was just like riding a bike. Nope, not at all. It's a different ride altogether. While going from having no shooting experience to taking your first shot could happen on the same day, the next day you still need that adult to come along and steady your experience—to remind you of the proper way to pick up the gun, to hold the gun, to pull the trigger.

135

There's so much to remember. It could take dozens of hours before you are shooting on your own, unsupervised.

Even after you complete a few hundred shooting hours, you'll notice you'll feel a little rusty when you return to the range after being away for a few months.

So get the right training to start and then get ongoing training to sharpen your skills.

Chris Luebkin, president and lead instructor for Semper Paradis Solutions, has been a shooting instructor for years, training men and women. He noticed a few differences in how men and women show up for class. He says more women than men show up nervous and scared at the start of his class.

But an amazing thing happens during the course: he sees these women transform from being unsure of themselves to showing up with confidence. It eventually helps women have "command presence"—it's that next level of confidence when you are not intimidated and will stand up for yourself in everyday situations.

You suddenly become more aware. You start thinking about an exit strategy. If you go to a restaurant, you notice where the exits are, you don't sit with your back facing a door. It's all about awareness of your surroundings—you'll hear this referred to as situational awareness. You think about how you'll respond.

There are benefits beyond gaining shooting ability sisters—you will gain heightened awareness and confidence!

Group Training

Should you take group lessons or individual lessons? An advantage to group training is that you can learn from others and meet a whole new group of people who have the same interest as you.

This isn't an either or. Get both group and individual training, because there are benefits to both.

WOMEN'S GROUPS

A huge benefit women have in the shooting world is they are natural helpers and want to share. We bring our nurturing skills to the group, making other women feel at home. We've all been there. New. Not wanting to look stupid.

Get over yourself. Everyone will know you are new to shooting by the way you act, what you say, and what you wear. Own it. Say aloud, I am new. Can you help me? Of course, we will!

The best place to ask these questions is in a women's group lesson because being in a group of women helps us feel safe enough to be vulnerable and helps you be okay with making mistakes, asking questions, and admitting you are a beginner.

Training for women is a focus of development for gun clubs and sellers. Do a quick internet search in your area for small meetups or gun clubs. Besides group lessons, you can also find women's shooting clubs and groups.

As an example, C2 Tactical in Arizona has a women's only club called Women of Steel which started in 2014, which has now grown to include 150 women.

C2's Senior Manager of Marketing, Membership, and Events, Gena Wagoner, said the group holds monthly meetings that include one hour in class and one hour of drills. They offer three-tiered women-only classes to choose from, depending on your level of experience, and you're welcome to take the mixed courses too, some of which are marksmanship, defensive shooting, and concealed carry. Wagoner recommends an all-women group over mixed group training because it's less intimidating with less judgement and a lot of camaraderie.

If you don't know where to begin, Wagoner recommends an intro to firearms class—which they offer for $60. You don't need a pistol for it, so it's perfect for beginners.

Women of Steel trains women in real-world scenarios too. Wagoner says it's important if you are going to concealed carry that you sometimes train wearing what you'd typically wear every day—that could be a dress and heels. The kick from the gun is going to rock you more in a pair of heels than in your flat athletic shoes, and you need to know how to handle that.

"Bottom line, this group is awesome and has great goals," Wagoner says, "It makes me feel good that women are taking responsibility. If I can keep one woman from being a victim, then that's success." Amen to that, sister.

Another reason to take an all-women class is we learn differently. "Women learn differently—female shooters are really good out-of-the-gate and more open to taking instruction. We listen. Guys think they know everything already," says Wagoner.

Oh, but we women can be haughty and catty, can't we? If you find yourself in a group like that, keep looking. You need to find a group that will help you, nurture you. After you've been doing this for a while, go back to that first group and show them a thing or two!

Individual Training

For women who are really scared or have specific things they want to work on, individual training can be a good way to go.

Individual instruction can put you on the fastback to becoming a better shooter. A benefit of going to an individual instructor when you are new to shooting is that you won't learn bad habits that you have to spend time undoing later.

If you are one-on-one, you are moving at your pace instead of at the pace of the class. Along the way, your instructor can tailor the training to your ability—spending more time where you need and less time where you don't need.

I recommend starting both individual and group instruction around the same time; you'll maximize the learning experience and compress the learning curve.

IMPORTANCE OF HAVING A GOOD INSTRUCTOR

When I sought out a gun instructor, I wanted to regain confidence. My partner at the time became an emotional bully, acting erratically and had an intimidating temper. This change set in gradually until one day while crying alone in my closet, I felt like I didn't know him anymore. It was as if aliens hovered over our house with the mothership and abducted the man I loved and replaced him with a temporary shell of a man. I was beaten down emotionally and had very low self-esteem. And trust me, that wasn't the only time I cried in my closet.

I tried counseling, self-help books, and they helped for sure. Those things helped explain what I was going through, but something was missing; I still didn't feel safe.

Then I remembered the sense of power I had when I shot for the very first time, so I thought I'd try that. The only person I knew who could teach me to shoot was my partner—you know—the one who was an emotional bully? No way. Instead, I went to the local gun club and hired an instructor. I never met him, I didn't know his background, and I sure didn't know what questions to ask. I only knew that he was on the club's list of instructors. Bottom line, I was clueless.

This man was critical, large in stature, and all business. The part I remember the most was him teaching me to breathe when I aimed. He said to pull the trigger on a slow exhale. I held my breath a lot rather than exhaling. He made me nervous, so I tensed up and that caused me to hold my breath. Looking back, I was a little afraid of him too because he had the intensity of my partner. I couldn't concentrate. And then I became self-conscious and had false starts. I would aim, and right before pulling the trigger, this waive of self-doubt would run through my body and out my outstretched arms. It caused me to reflexively lower the gun a hair but not shoot! I started anticipating the shot. I was all up in my head. Agh! It was so frustrating. The more I tried to concentrate, the worse was my aim. After a few lessons, at least I hit the target, and some of the hits were in the same area.

After a few more lessons, he told me that I had a tight grouping. I puffed up and thought, How about that; I have a tight grouping! No one has ever said that to me before! Umm, what is a grouping? I was wearing tight jeans, was he a perv? Tight grouping?

He explained to me that a grouping is when your shots are all nearby on the target. Oh, OK, good to know. No need to call the authorities. You want a tight grouping, assuming your grouping is in the area you want!

Then he said I was ready. He recommended I get a 9mm Kahr. It wasn't a gun that I shot with him, but he was sure that was the perfect gun for me. I filled out the form and turned it in for my background check, and that's when the gravity of this decision hit me. I was buying a gun. Me. I didn't know any other woman who owned a gun. Weren't they for boys?

Remember, I mentioned it was not the right gun for me and notice the Kahr is missing from the chapter on my gun reviews. Ugh! I bought this gun before ever shooting it, no research, and on the recommendation of someone I knew for 10 hours (10 lessons).

So, that Kahr rested in my safe for several months, and then I sold it back to the gun store.

He wasn't a good instructor for me.

How to choose the best instructor

Hiring a gun instructor is not something to take lightly. Hiring the wrong instructor could amplify any apprehension you're feeling and could teach you bad habits you have to break later.

I've read it takes about 1,000 repetitions to create muscle memory, and that's a lot of practice for your trigger technique to become second nature. But muscle memory is not expertise. You get where I'm going here? You can pull the trigger 1,000 times the *wrong* way. Practice does not equal perfect. Therefore, it's important as a beginning shooter that you're trained by an expert.

The problem with muscle memory is that it's hard to forget. So, if you learn the wrong way, I'd bet it takes 3,000 reps to correct the wrong, learn the right, and reestablish muscle memory for your trigger pull.

So first you need to learn the right way through a good instructor who builds up your confidence while building up your skills. A good instructor listens to you and teaches you what you need to know to get to the next level.

Women don't typically have the upper-body strength, so their arms fatigue faster than men's arms, so you want someone who is cognizant of that and factors that in the amount of time spent training at one time. Now, that is a sign of a good instructor. Meet your student where they're at.

That, my friends, is why finding the right instructor is something you should spend time on—don't do what I did and choose the instructor because he worked at the local gun club.

So then, how do you choose the best instructor for you? You are unique. The reason you want to shoot is your reason. What you want to get out of it is up to you. Use the questions and guidance below to help you make your choice.

None of these questions are a make or break—combine all of them to make your decision. Add to them to be sure your own needs are met. Use them to evaluate a group or private instructor.

WHAT QUALIFICATIONS DO YOU HAVE?

You'll first want to know what kind of certifications this person has. The most recognized credential is the NRA Instructor certification. Have they been trained or are they a really good shooter who wants to earn some money? How long have they been training others? A person may only have been training for a year, but prior to that they had been informally training friends and family and relying on referrals. There's not necessarily anything wrong with that, and it's okay to ask the question.

HOW OFTEN DO YOU SHOOT?

How many rounds a year do they shoot? This will let you know if they have a passion for it. People with passion try harder. A good guideline is 10,000 rounds per year.

HOW MANY WOMEN HAVE YOU TRAINED?

Now, the answer here is very important and may require some follow up. If they say none, ask them what they think the differences are between training men and women. That's a darn good question to ask regardless of their answer. This is going to reveal bias and stereotypes.

WILL I BE SHOOTING RIGHT AWAY?

If you already know the basics of shooting and one of your goals is to learn to be a shooter, you want hands-on training on the first day.

WHAT ARE YOUR FAVORITE HANDGUNS TO SHOOT?

This is good to ask up front rather than down the line when you are ready to buy. Chances are, they will steer you toward guns they shoot and like. Not necessarily bad, just another thing to be aware of.

IS THEIR STYLE COMPATIBLE WITH YOURS?

As I said, I learn best through positive encouragement, not criticism. And maybe you like detailed explanations of things but during your interview, they gloss over the details and instead generalize. That won't work for you.

WHAT IS THE COST?

In Arizona, the average cost is $80 per session. Sessions are usually an hour.

I created a checklist for you on the next page that you can take with you to interview any instructor. This will show them you are a serious student. For anyone who won't spend 10 minutes with you to be interviewed, you gotta pull a Taylor Swift, and—Next!

TOP 10 QUESTIONS TO ASK
before hiring an instructor -

INSTRUCTOR: _____

CERTIFICATIONS	
YEARS EXPERIENCE TRAINING	
FREQUENCY SHOOTING	
NUMBER OF WOMEN TRAINED	
WILL I SHOOT ON THE FIRST DAY?	
FAVORITE HANDGUNS	
STYLE COMPATIBLE	
CLEAR JAMS/ TRAINING ROUNDS	
CAN I ACCOMPLISH MY GOAL?	
COST	

Downloadable from handgunsforher.com.

Bonus: Strengthening Exercises

Betcha didn't think there'd be a fitness section in this book about handguns, did you? Well, here it is.

I noticed some of my muscles were sore after an afternoon of shooting, and I can tell you that shooting can be an upper-body workout. If you're super fit, you probably won't notice it, but if you don't work out your upper body regularly, don't be surprised. The stronger your upper-body strength, the more you'll enjoy shooting.

So even before you start shooting regularly, you can start today to get your muscles ready.

Here are some of my personal strengthening tips. (Always consult with your doctor or fitness expert before starting any exercise program.)

FRANKIE FIREARM FITNESS FIVE, OR F5. (YEAH, I MADE THAT NAME UP JUST NOW!)

F5 Tip #1—Hold both of your hands out in front of you like you're Frankenstein. Now, rotate your hands so your thumbs are at the top, pinkie at the bottom. This is roughly the position you'll be in when shooting. Try to engage your shoulders. Hold that pose until you start feeling it in our muscles. Are your biceps burning? How about your shoulders? You'll be using these muscles while shooting.

F5 Tip #2—There's probably an official fitness term for these, but I call then half curls. Start holding a weight in each hand with your arms straight in front of you like Frankenstein again, and then curl them up toward your shoulders. Full curls are good too, but these will work your biceps and your back. Do these with your wrists facing down, and then with your wrists facing up.

F5 Tip #3—For this next one, you're simulating pulling back the slide. The slide is at the top of the pistol, and as you pull back the top, you push the base in the opposite direction. Grab a tight exercise band and loop the band around your right palm (assuming you are right-hand dominant) so the loop is resting between your thumb and forefinger. Now get in your Frankie pose with arms in front. Grip the band with the left hand and push it out to the right in a slide motion. You'll want to choke up on the band so there's only about an inch worth of stretch. Experiment with moving the position of your hands from directly in front to slightly to the right while pulling. If you're doing it right, you'll feel this in your left bicep, deltoid, and pectorals.

F5 Tip #4—Sit in a chair, resting your lower forearm on your knees. Grip some light dumbbells with palms facing down. Then bend your wrist back, like a mini-curl. Then do the same thing with your palms facing up. If you can comfortably lean over an ironing board, that works too. If you have a forearm gripper, use that.

F5 Tip #5—Grab a tennis ball, racquetball, or dog ball in your hand. Squeeze it using your whole hand. Then isolate your index finger and squeeze it. Then isolate your thumb and squeeze it. This works your trigger finger and grip.

And let's not forget stretching. Hold your dominant hand in front of you, palm down. Bend back your fingers with your opposite hand. Hold for five seconds. Repeat. Next, put your dominant hand in a position like your hitchhiking. Bend your thumb back, toward your forearm. Hold for five seconds, repeat. That relieves tightness and helps your hand from cramping. I'm not a fitness expert, but these are moves that helped me.

You can start today with these exercises before you head to the range. The more prepared you are physically, the more fun you'll have.

Typically, women don't have the upper-body strength that men do, but that doesn't mean we aren't strong enough or can't become strong enough to be effective shooters. Now, have fun with your Frankie Five!

CHAPTER 12

ENTERING THE RANGE
WITH CONFIDENCE

Ranges are either very basic with shooting lanes and a small retail area or more elaborate ones complete with a shopping area, shooting area, shooting lanes, training areas, and sometimes an exclusive lounge. These elaborate ranges are called "gun clubs." According to the *Environmental Health Journal*, the **National Center for Biotechnology Information reported** 16,000–18,000 indoor firing ranges in the United States.[18]

You don't need to be a member to shoot at a gun club. However, being a member offers additional benefits: retail discounts, rental discounts on firearms and eyes and ears protection, and you get bumped up in the line of people waiting to shoot. Weekends are busy, and you can expect to wait. If it's your first time shooting there, they will require you to view a short safety video and sign a waiver. Watch the video and pay attention. This is not the time to upload selfies to Insta #firsttimeshooting.

Tip: There are two safety doors, and you must wait for one to close before you can pass through the other one.

Costs vary. Some charge one price for all day, while others charge hourly.

What to Bring

You don't need to bring a lot with you to the range. In fact, less is better because there won't be a lot of room to store things in your shooting lane area. I recommend bringing a wallet instead of a large purse. Certainly, if you are bringing a gun, bring it in a gun case, unloaded. Otherwise, you just need an ID, payment method, and hearing and eye protection if you have your own; these are also available for rent.

When you arrive, you will check in at the counter—have your driver's license ready.

HEARING PROTECTION

When you get to the range, they will ask you if you have hearing protection since you have to wear hearing protection at all times in the shooting area. Some ranges have these available for rent—check online or call in advance.

You also have the option of buying them there or bringing your own.

First, a bit about what level of hearing protection you need. On some ranges, handguns are allowed in the same area as their much louder cousins—rifles and machine guns.

Sound is measured in decibels, or dB. Normal conversation level is 60–70 dB. A nightclub with music is 110 dB according to OSHA, while a gunshot is above 140 dB. The American Speech-Language-Hearing Association says that exposure to noise greater than 140 dB can permanently damage hearing. Nearly all shots fired will be above this rating. When you add the reverberation that occurs with indoor shooting, whether at home or the range, you increase your chances for hearing loss.

Decibels by caliber

The average dB noise levels for calibers according to USA Carry:[19]

.22 Pistol or Rifle—140 dB
380—157.7 dB
9mm—159.8 dB
38 S&W—153.5 dB
38 Spl—156.3 dB
357 Magnum—164.3 dB
40 S&W—156.5 dB
45 ACP—157.0 dB
45 COLT—154.7 dB
12 Gauge Shotgun—155 dB
M-16—160 dB

Costs

Electronic hearing protection devices (HPDs) range in cost from $100 for earmuffs to over $1,000 for high-technology custom-made devices. Insert plug-type nonlinear HPDs cost around $10–$20, while custom-made nonlinear devices cost around $100–$150 per pair.

Options

Noise Reduction Rating (NRR) is the hearing protection rating method used in the US. NRR is important because it indicates the functionality of a device and the ability of that device to protect your hearing.

The higher the NRR, the greater protection. The highest NRR you can get in a single device is 35. You'll want to look for a rating of 28–31 if you're shooting indoors.

Read the packaging of your hearing protection gear as it will list a range of protection given, and this range depends on the fit to the individual user.

The wider the range, the more variable the fit.

One hearing protection option is earplugs. Personally, I don't think that over the counter ones offer enough protection.

I opted to get hot wax poured in my ears for custom earplugs. Okay, it wasn't hot, and certainly not as painful as a Brazilian, but it was a little warm and weird feeling. But these custom earplugs are made to the exact shape of your ear canal!

I was afraid to get it done at first. I mean, what's stopping the wax from going all the way to the bottom of my ear canal and never coming out again?

You sit in a chair and they pour it in. You hardly feel it. It sits there for a short time, and then they pull it out. Oh, but before that, you get to choose colors. There are many options here, ladies, even hot pink. You'll want to get two different colors; one for your right ear, one for your left. It's just easier to identify which goes in which ear. Did you know your ear canals are not identical? So you have to use the right one for the right ear.

The plugs are awkward to use at first, so rotate each slightly as you put it in your ear. And trust me, you can't put them in the wrong ear. It slides in and fits perfectly. No danger of these falling out like there could be with plugs you get over the counter.

Keep these in the case and clean them regularly. It's also important to keep your ears clear of ear wax; otherwise, the plugs push down the buildup.

Pro tip: Before getting fitted for wax earplugs, go to a professional to get your ears cleared of any wax or use wax remover at home a few times beforehand. Have you ever seen what was removed from your ears in the doctor's office? It is truly one of the wonders of the world, but not in a good way. I had it done and what he pulled out of there was terrifying.

Let's look at some of your other hearing protection options.

Passive earplugs: these are the kind you can easily find at a drugstore or big box store. This is your go-to if you have a partner who snores, or you travel a lot and need to block out the hallway sounds at the hotels.

Passive hearing protection: think ear muffs that are attached to a band that fits over your head and the muff cups your ear. These provide a good level of ear protection but the drawback is you need to become pretty good at reading lips—they also block the voices of anyone you are shooting with. Think headphones from the 80s. They are big.

Electronic Noise-cancelling hearing protection: this is the ear muff style on steroids. It blocks harmful noise, but lets you hear conversations. The downside is that it is the most expensive option. If you can afford it, this offers the best protection. This will set you back starting at $250. I'm practical and unless you are shooting more than once a week, hold off on this big purchase until you have a fair amount of shooting hours under your belt.

I have sensitive ears so I wear earplugs and bring outside ear protection—looks like headphones—to put over them in case there are rifles or machine guns in other lanes nearby. What can I say, I value my hearing. And it's a recommended practice by the American Speech-Language-Hearing Association if you are exposed to firing of calibers with a diameter of .40 inches or larger.

EYE PROTECTION

Just like with hearing protection, some ranges offer eye protection for rent. Or you can buy your own. Even if you wear eyeglasses regularly, wear larger eye protection over them to protect them from shattering and cutting your eye. Do not think large sunglasses are proper protection. Do not wear anything that darkens your surroundings. This is a time to be 100 percent aware of what you and others around you are doing.

You will likely have shell casings hit your glasses, your face, and your upper body. At first, you may flinch, but after time, they won't be much of a distraction. Whatever you do, if you get tapped by the brass, *always keep the gun pointed downrange.*

I recommend visiting the range before your first time shooting to ease some of the jitters you may have.

SMALL PURSE

That big purse that also subs as a diaper bag needs to be left in the car. Bring a wallet or a very small purse. Each shooter or group of shooters is assigned a lane, and it's a pretty narrow, without much room to store things. I'd bring a small purse that can hold your wallet, ear and eye protection, and your phone.

IN REVIEW

Bring the following:

- Driver's license or state-issued ID. You don't need a gun license to shoot at a range.

- Cash/credit card to pay for your range time, target rentals, or hearing and eye protection rentals (if you aren't bringing your own).

- Range bag, small wallet, or purse to carry your ID, phone, cash, or a credit card.

- Ear and eye protection.

Range Rules and Etiquette

Check the rules at the shooting range before you go. I wouldn't expect anything out of the ordinary; it's just good practice.

- Mind-altering substances (drugs or alcohol) are not allowed inside or outside the body.

- Do not carry a loaded gun into the range.

- Bring your gun to the range in a case.

- Always listen and obey the Range Officer (RO).

- Treat all firearms as if they are loaded.

- Never point a firearm at anything you are not willing to destroy.

- Keep your finger off the trigger and out of the trigger guard until you are on target and ready to fire.

- Always identify your target as well as what is beyond and around it.

- Wear eye and ear protection.

- If you aren't shooting, stand 1–2 yards behind the shooter.

- Do not cross the bright red/yellow line in front of the shooting table.

If you see someone doing something unsafe, report them to the range master immediately—these are the staff standing in the back ensuring everyone's safety.

Again, ladies, go with your gut, your intuition. Even if you haven't seen something unsafe, if you don't feel safe, it could be that that female brain of yours has picked up on something subtle about someone next to you, so ask to move to another lane or leave the range altogether. If the range isn't busy, they will accommodate you. If they are busy, then you'll wait.

Safety above all else.

SAFETY OVER SELFIES

Shooting a handgun is a big deal for first-timers. Shooting a new gun, especially an automatic rifle, for the first time is an even bigger deal. So people want to take selfies. Nearly 70 percent of the time I go to the range, someone is doing a different kind of shooting: they're shooting a video of their friend shooting. This makes me nervous, to be honest, because I wonder if they are paying more attention to the selfie than to the safety.

If you are taking a video or photo, take it then put your phone away. A couple of things about using your cell phone. Do not remove your range goggles to get a better view of the phone screen. Notice where the shell casings are falling, and don't stand in their path. Don't ask anyone in other lanes to take your photo or video. This is just bad etiquette.

BE CAREFUL OF THE SHELL CASINGS

After shooting several rounds, you'll see shell casings behind you, under you, and you may even be stepping on them. Have you ever gone to a bar where they serve peanuts and you can drop the shells on the floor? It reminds me of that. The peanut shells are all over and you step on them.

I like to keep a clean area, so I grab the squeegee thing with the handle at the back of the room, and I push empty shell casings in front of my shooting area, right onto the lane. This way I can be sure my feet will be grounded on the floor and not teetering on a piece of metal.

What to Wear

Is your man going to tell you what to wear to the gun range? Ah, that's a big no. What do you think he'll wear? A t-shirt, jeans, and sneakers? Probably.

But will your best girlfriend tell you what to wear? You bet.

And here's what she'd say if you asked her what to wear to the shooting range — *Leave the cleavage at home, sister!*

One afternoon at the range, I looked to my right and saw a guy and a girl in the next lane. The girl wore tight jeans and heels and a very form-fitting top, with more than a tease of cleavage. *Eye roll* I've seen this show before.

I thought, her guy didn't tell her what to wear, and it's only a matter of time before she learns on her own.

I went back to shooting and waiting for the electronic arm to return my obliterated target when out of the corner of my eye, I saw some fast movement.

Bam! She was reaching down and bending over at the same time to get the hot brass from between her breasts. Ouch, ouch, ouch. You never forget the first time brass gets trapped between your skin and your clothes. It feels a lot like a hot curling iron against your neck, wound tightly around your hair, and you can't release it fast enough.

Don't believe me? Go ahead, wear your sexy low-cut top and be sure to let me know if you are permanently scarred or just singed.

Instead of your sexy low-cut top, wear something with a crew neck. Wearing short or long sleeves doesn't matter much, but if you wear long sleeves, just be sure they aren't billowy sleeves— that extra fabric can get caught on something and tear.

No white clothing either, unless it's an old t-shirt. Guns are dirty. Plus, you're touching ammo and that's dirty too. As in her case, sometimes that brass hits you and leaves a mark.

SHOES

Ever dropped something on your toe? Something with a sharp edge? Your toe can literally get nicked from the brass. Yikes, that hurts. So no sandals. It may be hot outside, but inside, these ranges are kept cool, so your feet will end up being cold and nicked. I recommend sneakers or something sturdy like hiking boots. If you want to be somewhat fashionable, wear fashion boots with a chunky heel.

And please, forgetto the stiletto. This is outright dangerous for beginner shooters. What happens is that after several rounds are shot, you have a lot of brass on the ground behind you. It's like walking on small landscaping stones. Step on one wrong, and the heel twists, and so do you. If you're lucky, you recover; at worst, you land on your ass, humiliated, and God forbid, you sprain your shooting hand! Or you go down with the gun in your hand. Yikes. Whatever shoes you choose, be sure they are closed-toe. Save the stilettos for a time after you're more familiar with shooting. Need one more reason to wear close-toed shoes? Protect that nice pedicure you have.

NAIL IT!

This is one place where it's okay to have short nails and a manicure that's two weeks old. There are so many reasons why sculpted long nails and guns are a bad combo. First, you are guaranteed to ruin a fresh manicure: metal + nails = nicks. Second, the way you grip the gun, your fingers wrap around and your nails can gouge into your hand. Yeah, I speak from experience. Third, it's darn hard to load cartridges into the magazine with long nails!

When You Leave

Before you leave your lane, unload your gun, clean up around your area, throw out your used target—or keep it it's something you're proud of, be sure your weapons are unloaded and packed in the case or bag they came in, and use the long-handled squeegee to push your empty shell casings forward into the firing lanes. (The squeegee is likely leaning against the wall behind the lanes.)

Before you leave the facility, head to the restroom and wash your hands. Guns are dirty. I wash my hands twice because there's so much grime. If you pulled out your phone during your session, clean your phone too.

Then, walk to the back of the room—do not cut close behind other shooters—and walk out.

Oh, one thing about walking out. Ranges are set up to have a double door safety. There's a button on the wall you press—looks like the buttons for handicapped accessible doors. It opens the door, and then you step into a breezeway and wait for the door to close. If you want to really give away that you're a newbie, press the button for the next door before the first door is closed. It won't work because the doors are set up so they can't be both opened at the same time.

Have fun at the range. Shooting can be a really exhilarating outing that should be enjoyed. *Never put fun above safety.*

CONCLUSION

PARTING SHOTS

Congratulations, you are well on your way to protecting yourself and loved ones by being a responsible gun owner!

Gun ownership will help you defend yourself and your loved ones. You've learned how to choose the right gun for you, how to get the right training, and to enter the range with confidence.

And, I promise the insider tips you got here propelled you well beyond other women who are beginner shooters!

I wish I could be there with you when you get your first tight grouping. You'll be beaming. You'll have flashbacks of when you were five and you were so proud of that art project you did at school that you ran all the way home with the paper waving it like a kite, burst in the door, and said, "Look what I did!" Yeah, it will be like that.

So, when you get those first tight groupings, set your gun down, reel in the target, look at it close, smile, look around, make sure other people see it, then take it down, and tuck it away. Keep that. That's your art project. Take it home and stick it on your fridge. Celebrate your victories along your journey.

Now, the next step in your journey is up to you. You get to write the next chapter. You picked up this book for a reason. Take action now, so you won't be huddled in the closet, defenseless if someone breaks into your home. Make your next chapter one of victory, not victimhood!

You are an empowered, beautiful woman—I am proud of you for taking the next step!

Download my handgun ranking sheet and instructor assessment form at handgunsforher.com.

GLOSSARY

Ammunition—Projectiles with fuses and primers fired from guns.

Brass—A term for fired cartridge cases. This is what can bounce off your face or get stuck in your cleavage if you're not careful. Brass can refer to brass or steel cases.

Blank—a type of cartridge for a firearm that contains gunpowder but no bullet or shot. Blanks use paper or plastic wadding to seal gunpowder into the cartridge. When fired, the blank makes a flash and an explosive sound—like a cap gun.

Bullet—a component of a cartridge.

Caliber—the diameter of the ammunition. Sometimes measured in millimeters (ex. 9mm) and sometimes measured in hundreds of an inch (ex. .22).

Cartridge—what we commonly, and incorrectly refer to as the bullet. Cartridges consist of the case, primer, propellant, and projectile.

Chamber—the place the cartridge sits in the gun all cozy until the gun is fired. There's only room for one cartridge in the chamber. To chamber a round means to load a cartridge into the chamber.

Clip—it holds ammo and loads magazines on rifles. Sometimes people say clip but they mean magazine.

Cylinder—the chamber on a revolver.

Concealed carry—Carrying any weapon that is not easily noticeable to the average person.

Dry fire—Dry firing is simply the practice of shooting a firearm without ammunition in the chamber. The user pulls the trigger, the hammer drops, but nothing happens. Great for practice.

Federal Firearms License (FFL)—the document that allows an individual or company to buy, sell, or manufacture firearms in the US. FFLs are issued and monitored by the ATF. It also refers to the people who hold the FFL. FFLs are contacted by the ATF if a question is raised about a gun that is involved with a crime.

Grain—The term grains refers to the projectile's mass or weight. There are 437.5 grains in an ounce. It refers to the mass of the bullet itself, not the entire cartridge—just the projectile.

Grip—The part of the gun that you hold while shooting. It helps you aim and control the gun.

Grouping—the pattern on our target after shooting multiple rounds. A "tight" grouping is what you are going for if it's on the point on the target you intended.

Gun—the most general term for a firearm that shoots projectiles. It's a weapon incorporating a metal tube from which bullets, shells, or other missiles are propelled by explosive force, typically making a characteristic loud, sharp noise.

Hammer—The hammer is a part of a firearm that is used to strike the percussion cap/primer, or a separate firing pin, to ignite the propellant and fire the projectile. Oh, and it looks like a hammer.

Handgun—same definition as a pistol: a small firearm designed to be held in one hand. Except it does include pistols and revolvers.

Hot—yes, of course, I am referring to you! But also, this means when people are actively shooting as in "the range is hot."

Magazine—an ammunition storage and feeding device within or attached to a repeating firearm.

Pistol—a small firearm designed to be held in one hand. The ATF defines a pistol as any handgun that does not contain its ammunition in a revolving cylinder. Otherwise, it would be known as a revolver!

Revolver—a handgun having a revolving chambered cylinder for holding several cartridges, which may be discharged in succession without reloading.

Range—A place you go to shoot. Can be indoors or outdoors.

Recoil—How much your gun sasses back. The recoil of a gun is a backward movement caused by shooting a round. Usually, the larger the gun and caliber, the greater the recoil.

Round—another name for a cartridge. A complete unit of ammunition that has a casing, a primer, a propellant, and a projectile.

Safety—A safety is a mechanical device that should prevent a firearm from firing when not engaged. A safety works by stopping the firing pin from striking the primer.

Semi-automatic—A semi-automatic firearm (also known as self-loading or autoloading) is one which automatically loads a following round of cartridge into the chamber and prepares it for subsequent firing, but requires the shooter to manually pull the trigger in order to discharge each shot.

Silencer—A device installed on the barrel of a firearm to reduce the report of a firearm. Controlled by the NFA and has the special $200 tax. They save your hearing!

Slide—runs the length of the pistil and can be pulled back. The slide is the part that moves during the operating cycle and generally houses the firing pin/striker and the extractor. Found on most semi-automatic pistols.

Trigger—the piece on the firearm that when pressed by the finger, actuates the mechanism that discharges the weapon, causing the cartridge to shoot.

Velocity—the speed the bullet travels when fired from a gun.

COMMON GUN FEATURES

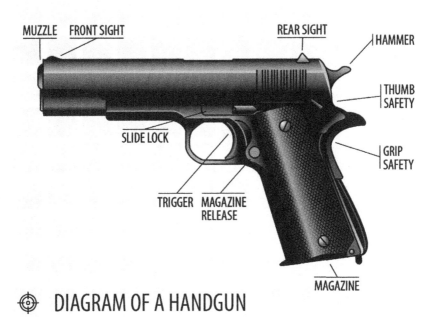

⊕ DIAGRAM OF A HANDGUN

REFERENCES

[1] Halpin, Matt. "What Is The Average Police Response Time In The US?" *A Secure Life,* January 29, 2019,

https://www.asecurelife.com/average-police-response-time/

[2] Pagones, Stephanie. "Gun Sales Break May Record Amid Coronavirus Pandemic, Riots," *Yahoo! News*, June 2, 2020,

https://www.yahoo.com/news/gun-sales-break-may-record-202149954.html?guccounter=1

[3] Crime and Justice News, "IL Gun Sales Up 500%; Many First-Time Buyers, Women," *The Crime Report*, June 26, 2020,

https://thecrimereport.org/2020/06/26/il-gun-sales-up-500-many-first-time-buyers-women/

[4] Edward, Susanne. "The RISE Of The Woman Gun Owner," *America's First Freedom*, The National Rifle Association, January 11, 2020,

https://www.americas1stfreedom.org/articles/2020/1/11/the-rise-of-the-woman-gun-owner/

[5] Horowitz, Juliana M. "How Male And Female Gun Owners In The U.S. Compare," *Pew Research Center*, June 29, 2017,

https://www.pewresearch.org/fact-tank/2017/06/29/how-male-and-female-gun-owners-in-the-u-s-compare/

[6] "America Has Added 2 MILLION First-Time Gun Owners In Five Months, Including 800,000 Women," *2nd Amendment Daily News*, May 2020,

https://www.secondamendmentdaily.com/2020/06/america-has-added-2-million-first-time-gun-owners-in-five-months-including-800000-women/

[7] Pagones, Stephanie. "Gun Sales Break May Record Amid Coronavirus Pandemic, Riots," *Fox Business*, June 2, 2020, https://www.foxbusiness.com/lifestyle/gun-sales-may-record-coronavirus-riots

[8] "What Qualifies As A Secure Gun Storage Or Safety Device?" Bureau Of Alcohol, Tobacco, Firearms and Explosives, September 10, 2015, https://www.atf.gov/firearms/qa/what-qualifies-secure-gun-storage-or-safety-device

[9] Parker, Kim, Juliana M. Horowitz, Ruth Igielnik, J. Oliphant, and Anna Brown. "America's Complex Relationship With Guns," *Pew Research Center's Social & Demographic Trends Project*, June 22, 2017, https://www.pewsocialtrends.org/2017/06/22/americas-complex-relationship-with-guns/

[10] Laidlaw, Mark A S et al. "Lead exposure at firing ranges—a review." *Environmental Health* 16, no 34 (April 2017):1, https://doi.org/10.1186/s12940-017-0246-0

[11] "Loud Noise Dangers," American Speech-Language-Hearing Association, accessed October 2020, https://www.asha.org/public/hearing/loud-noise-dangers/

[12] Igielnik, Ruth and Anna Brown. "Americans' Views On Guns And Gun Ownership: 8 Key Findings," *Pew Research Center*, June 22, 2017, https://www.pewresearch.org/fact-tank/2017/06/22/key-takeaways-on-americans-views-of-guns-and-gun-ownership/

REFERENCES

13 "Second Amendment," Legal Information Institute, 2020, https://www.law.cornell.edu/wex/second_amendment

14 "Basic Carry Laws: Arizona," *Born to Protect* (blog), February 2, 2020, https://www.usconcealedcarry.com/blog/basic-carry-laws-arizona/

15 "Gun Policy Remains Divisive, but Several Proposals Still Draw Bipartisan Support," Pew Research Center, October 18, 2018, https://www.pewresearch.org/politics/2018/10/18/gun-policy-remains-divisive-but-several-proposals-still-draw-bipartisan-support/

16 Peterson, Jillian and James Densley. "We have studied every mass shooting since 1966. Here's what we learned about the shooters," *Los Angeles Times*, August 4, 2019, https://www.latimes.com/opinion/story/2019-08-04/el-paso-dayton-gilroy-mass-shooters-data

17 "What is My Hand Size?" The Center for Construction Research and Training, https://choosehandsafety.org//choosing-hand-tools/hand-tool-size

18 Laidlaw, Mark A S et al. "Lead exposure at firing ranges—a review." *Environmental Health* 16, no 34 (April 2017):1, https://doi.org/10.1186/s12940-017-0246-0

19 Findley, Ben. "Select Proper Hearing Protection For Shooting To Avoid Permanent Hearing Loss," *USA Carry*, January 3, 2013, https://www.usacarry.com/select-proper-hearing-protection-for-shooting-to-avoid-permanent-hearing-loss/

Made in the USA
Monee, IL
30 September 2024

66858546R00105